Markets or Governments

D1637003

Markets or Governments

Choosing between Imperfect Alternatives

Second Edition

Charles Wolf, Jr.

A RAND Research Study

The MIT Press
Cambridge, Massachusetts
London, England

RAND books are available on a wide variety of topics. To receive a list of RAND books, write or call Distribution Services, RAND, 1700 Main Street, P.O. Box 2138, Santa Monica, CA 90407-2138, (310) 393-0411, ext. 6686.

ISBN 978-0-262-23172-5 (hc.) -- ISBN 978-0-262-73104-1 (pbk)

Library of Congress Cataloging-in-Publications Data

Wolf, Charles, 1924–
  Markets or governments : choosing between imperfect alternatives / Charles Wolf, Jr.—2nd ed.
    p. cm.
  Includes bibliographical references and index.

  1. Capitalism. 2. Economic Policy. I. Title.
HB501.W89 1993
338.9—dc20

The MIT Press is pleased to keep this title available in print by manufacturing single copies, on demand, via digital printing technology.

To Nathan Leites

Friend and colleague,
without whose stimulus,
encouragement, and
insistence this book would
not have been written

Contents

Figures and Tables

Preface

Although markets are really what economics is all about, economists, as well as other social scientists and policy analysts, often display a profound ambivalence toward them. On the one hand, the virtues of perfect markets are extolled, as reflected in the core of microeconomic price theory. On the other hand, the market's manifest shortcomings have been amply codified in the formal "theory of market failure."

Surprisingly, economists and economics have been much less effective in addressing the predictable shortcomings and miscarriages of government and of government efforts to remedy the market's shortcomings. This book tries to redress the imbalance, by developing a framework for analyzing and anticipating the shortcomings of government. The framework—the "theory of *nonmarket* failure"—provides a basis for comparison and choice between markets and governments.

This choice is complex and multifaceted. It is neither a choice between perfect markets and imperfect governments nor one between imperfect markets and perfect governments. Instead, it is a choice between imperfect markets and imperfect governments, as well as imperfect combinations between them.

My principal aim in this book is not to make the choice nor to argue the case for markets over governments or vice versa. Those arguments have been made elsewhere, and numerous references will be made to them. Instead, my intention is to suggest how the methods used in comparing the respective shortcomings (as well as merits) of markets and governments can be improved, thereby contributing, one hopes, to better evaluations and choices.

Toward this end, I start with the premise that the market's flaws have, in logical and analytical terms, been much more elaborately dissected than have the corresponding flaws of the "nonmarket"—that is, of government. To be sure, government certainly receives ample hostile and probing criticism, especially in the political arena. Nevertheless, although the criticism is often severe, it typically lacks the logic and structure that have long since undergirded the conventionally accepted expositions, in the economics literature especially, of the failures of the market. Consequently, my main goal is to redress this imbalance by advancing the analysis of nonmarket flaws closer to the level already reached in analyzing those of the market.

This book is the outgrowth of several previous journal articles and book chapters, especially "A Theory of Nonmarket Failure," *Journal of Law and Economics*, April 1979; "Economic Efficiency and Inefficient Economics," *Journal of Post-Keynesian Economics*, Fall 1979; "Ethics and Policy Analysis," in *Public Duties: The Moral Obligations of Government Officials* (J. Fleishman, L. Liebman, M. Moore, eds., 1981); "'Non-Market Failure' Revisited: The Anatomy and Physiology of Government Deficiencies," in *Anatomy of Government Deficiencies* (H. Hanusch, ed., 1983); "Government Shortcomings and the Conditions of Demand," in *Public Finance and the Quest for Efficiency* (H. Hanusch, ed., 1984); and "Getting to Market," in *The National Interest*, 1991. In revising and updating the earlier material, as well as in the new material included in this book, I have tried to reach general readers as well as economists. Most of the discussion is readily accessible to readers who have taken an elementary course in economics and are comfortable with economic discussions in, say, the *Wall Street Journal*, *Business Week*, and *Barron's*. I hope that the substantive discussion will hold the attention of professional economists, as well. With this mixed audience in mind, I have placed technical discussion either in appendixes at the end of the text or in notes at chapter ends.

Several revisions have been made in this second edition of *Markets or Governments*. These involve changes in references to the former Soviet Union and Eastern Europe to allow for the historic changes that have occurred in these countries, updating many of the examples and data relating to the United States, and adding several references to earlier literature that are relevant to the theory of nonmarket failure elaborated in this book. Apart from these revisions, the structure and argument of the 1988 edition remain unchanged and, in my judgment, essentially sound.

Acknowledgments

This book was part of a RAND project, "The Roles and Missions of Government and the Private Sector," supported by the Sloan Foundation and RAND. I thank several colleagues at RAND and The RAND Graduate School who have read and commented on some of the precursor articles and on seminars based on them. I am especially grateful to the late Nathan Leites, who strenuously urged me to do this book, and to whom the book is dedicated; Anthony Pascal, who made many invaluable comments on two earlier drafts, Will Harriss for editorial improvements; Juanita Sanders and Terry Halpern, who executed innumerable revisions, reorganizations, and recombinations of the materials for the book's first edition; Donna Betancourt and Joye Hunter for administrative assistance; and Brent Boultinghouse, a RAND Graduate School fellow, for research assistance in preparing the second edition.

Markets or
Governments

1   The Cardinal
Economic Choice

In 1977, John Kenneth Galbraith presented a television series entitled "The Age of Uncertainty." Two years later, Milton Friedman followed with a series entitled "Free to Choose," intended as a rebuttal to the Galbraith series, although, as in some election campaigns, the adversary was not mentioned explicitly. Both Galbraith (1977) and Friedman (Friedman and Friedman, 1980) produced best-selling books from their television scripts—thereby showing that the economic behavior of individuals may be the same even if their economic policies are not.

Age of Uncertainty and *Free to Choose* dealt with the same subject: the market economy—how it originated and evolved, how it functions, and its strengths and weaknesses. Both books presented the policy implications of this analysis with respect to the cardinal economic choice: that between the market and government as the predominant regulator of economic activity. There the resemblance between the two contestants ended.

While Galbraith, in the tradition of Marx and Schumpeter, fully acknowledged the accomplishments of the market, he identified its evolution and maturation with macroeconomic instability ("uncertainty"), microeconomic inefficiency, and social inequity. Although Galbraith shared the Schumpeterian and Marxian view of the dramatic economic and technological accomplishments of capitalism and the market, his evaluation of the efficiency and equity of the system was sharply different from that of Schumpeter (1934) and closer to that of Marx. To remedy these deficiencies of the market, Galbraith and *Age of Uncertainty* viewed government policy and intervention as essential to bringing about economic stability, efficiency, and enhanced social equity.

Friedman, in the tradition of Adam Smith's *Wealth of Nations*, viewed the salient characteristics of the market system very differently from Galbraith. According to Friedman, a freely functioning market economy results in economic and technological progress, efficient utilization of resources, a rising standard of living that, with certain acknowledged exceptions, is distributed with reasonable equity,[1] and a society characterized by social mobility and political freedom. In the view of Friedman and *Free to Choose*, expansion of government beyond its minimal ("public good") functions (e.g., defense and public order, but *not* the postal service) impairs efficient resource use, impedes economic progress, and restricts social mobility and ultimately political freedom as well.

What accounts for these two knowledgeable observers' sharply contrasting views of the market and government?

The promarket view, represented by Friedman, is based on an idealized model of a perfectly competitive market, which tends toward full employment equilibrium for the economy as a whole (the macroeconomy), and efficient use of resources by the firm and the individual (the microeconomy). This view draws support from the past century's experience of market economies in the industrialized West and Japan, the 1970s and 1980s experience of the predominantly market economies in the "newly industrialized countries" of Hong Kong, Malaysia, Singapore, South Korea, and Taiwan, and the more recent growth experience of increased marketization in Thailand and Indonesia. Friedman's stance against government intervention draws additional support from innumerable anecdotes about the propensity of large government organizations, wherever they may be, to mismanage their tasks (e.g., the post office, welfare agencies, defense, and nationalized industries), the persistently disappointing economic records of most Third World countries in which government intervention has been pervasive and, since the late 1980s, the collapse and dismantling of the centrally planned command economies of the former Soviet Union, East Germany, and Eastern Europe.

On the other hand, the progovernment view represented by Galbraith and *Age of Uncertainty* is based on an idealized model of an informed, efficient, and humane government, able to identify and remedy failures of the market and to achieve national goals arrived at by democratic means, in accord with the precepts of formal welfare economics, as elaborated by I. M. D. Little, Richard Musgrave, and others, and the theory of optimal economic planning developed by Oscar Lange and Abba Lerner. This view draws empirical support from the generally favorable economic performance of the Scandinavian countries and the Netherlands in the postWorld War II period (at least until the late 1970s, when their economic trends became less favorable), specific instances of efficient governmental performance such as Europe's national railway systems, and the dramatic record of Japan's sustained postwar economic growth attributed to guidance and targeting by government policy (Japan's experience is cited in support of *both* sides of the argument!). Similarly, the Galbraith stance against the market also draws support from anecdotes about such negative market externalities as atmospheric pollution, airport noise, advertising billboards, and the often low quality of commercial television.

It is significant that the antimarket view reflected by Galbraith is supported by a formal *theory* of market failure, which also constitutes the core of welfare economics. This theory elaborates the predictable shortcomings of markets when confronted with public goods, externalities, increasing returns to scale, market "imperfections" of various kinds, and the possible social inequity of even "efficient" market outcomesconditions that are found in all markets some of the time and some markets all of the time.[2] In its turn, welfare economics provides rules and guidelines for government intervention to remedy, or at least alleviate, these shortcomings. The progovernment view has also received more recent theoretical support from the writings of Paul Krugman and others dealing with potential externalities associated with "critical" technologies, and with government-supported research and development to advance them.

By contrast, the antigovernment view reflected by Friedman cannot lean for equivalent support on a formal theory of nonmarket failure. That theory does not exist.

Thus, an interesting asymmetry emerges in comparing the sources and types of support for the promarket/antigovernment intervention views of Friedman with the progovernment/antimarket views espoused by Galbraith. The asymmetry is represented by the shaded rectangle in figure 1.1; that is, the argument between the promarket/antigovernment and progovernment/antimarket positions tends to be unbalanced because we lack a comprehensive theory of government shortcomings ("nonmarket failures") as a counterpart to the existing theory of market failure. Lest the absence of suitable theory be dismissed as unimportant, it is worth recalling the comment of John Maynard Keynes: "Practical men, who believe themselves to be quite exempt from any intellectual influences, are usually the slaves of some defunct economist. . . . [The] power of vested interests

	Markets	**Governments (Nonmarket)**
Pro	Theory of competitive markets, supported by examples and country experience	Theory of planning and welfare economics, supported by examples and country experience
Anti	Theory of market failure, supported by examples and country experience	
		examples and country experience

Figure 1.1
Markets versus governments: sources of support and opposition.

is vastly exaggerated compared with the gradual encroachment of ideas." (Keynes, 1936)

A more fully developed theory of nonmarket failure would thus help to provide better balance in the figure 1.1 matrix, as well as a better guide to public policy. The aims of this book are to help in developing this theory and to suggest how the theory can be applied in comparing nonmarket and market alternativesthereby, one would hope, contributing to improved choices or combinations between them.

An important element in such a comprehensive theory of nonmarket failure is provided by public choice theory.[3] As public choice theory emphasizes, the self-interest of politicians and bureaucrats is an important factor in understanding nonmarket processes. Nevertheless, a complete theory of nonmarket failure requires more than is provided by public choice alone. For example, the typical pattern of exclusivity (monopoly) in the conduct of nonmarket activities, the high degree of uncertainty surrounding the technology of producing nonmarket outputs, and the frequency of derived or unanticipated externalities resulting from these outputs are ignored or inadequately explained by existing public choice theory. Moreover, public choice theory ignores the role of organizational inertia, tradition, and standard operating routines as contributors to nonmarket failures. These factors are even more likely to be influential in organizations insulated from the discipline of the market than in organizations (i.e., firms) that are subject to that discipline.

The needed theory should embrace the wider range of activities, outputs, and failures covered by the nonmarket sector as a whole, rather than the public (government) sector alone. Although government is the largest member of the nonmarket sector, the others (foundations, universities, and nonproprietary hospitals, for example) are numerous, vast, and growing. The behavior and deficiencies of those other nonmarket organizations should be included in a comprehensive theory of nonmarket failure that can highlight similarities and differences among them, as well as permit suitable comparisons to be made between the nonmarket sector and the market sector. Public choice theory, by itself, is too restricted to provide an adequate frame for this picture.[4]

Austrian economic theory—especially that associated with Friedrich von Hayek and Ludwig von Mises—provides another element that is valuable for developing a comprehensive theory of nonmarket failure. In their focus on market competition and the price mechanism as a "procedure" for generating information, as well as the incentives provided by private ownership in motivating this procedure, Hayek and Mises contended that markets possess crucial advantages that government (nonmarkets) cannot match.[5]

Oliver Williamson's significant work on "transaction cost economics" likewise contributes valuable insights for developing a theory of nonmarket failure. Indeed, both market failure and nonmarket failure can be viewed as resulting from the particular transaction cost characteristics and burdens associated, respectively, with markets and governments as alternative "governance structures" for organizing economic activities.[6]

The dispute between Friedman and Galbraith reflects the cardinal policy issue facing modern economic systems: What is the appropriate role of government and of the market in the functioning of the economic system? And what are the appropriate rules and considerations to be applied in making this choice? Moreover, the choice should not be dichotomized, as Galbraith and Friedman sometimes imply, as a choice between relatively perfect governments and imperfect or inadequate markets (the Galbraith view), or between relatively perfect markets and imperfect or inadequate governments (the Friedman view). The actual choice is among imperfect markets, imperfect governments, and various combinations of the two. The cardinal economic choice concerns the degree to which markets or governments—each with their respective flaws—should determine the allocation, use, and distribution of resources in the economy.

This cardinal issue pervades American politics as well as the economy. An ideological, as well as visceral, emotional, and intellectual, difference about the appropriate resolution of this issue is the principal division between the Republican and Democratic parties. The market versus government issue also typically divides the business and financial communities (promarket) from the media and academic communities (progovernment). All of these divisions are often blurred by the willingness of protagonists on both sides to adjust their principles to more immediate and practical considerations of self-interest.

Thus, the American business and financial communities, which characteristically extol the virtues of the market and contribute handsomely to the Republican party, are often in the forefront of lobbying activities favoring protection of domestic markets against competing imports produced with cheap foreign labor. Correspondingly, the academic and media communities, which typically extol the virtues of government intervention and usually contribute their words and efforts to the Democratic party, become hypersensitive if the governmental intervention and assistance that they favor is tied to standards or criteria pertaining to their own activities. For example, these groups often urge government aid to education, but oppose having it conditioned on standards of performance established and evaluated by government. Milton Friedman has aptly commented on this familiar subservience of principle to self-interest by observing that promarket advocates in industry seem to favor the market's free operation with regard to the functioning of other industries, while seeking government help for their own. On the other hand, progovernment advocates in academe favor freedom from government restraint for their own activities, while advocating enlightened government intervention to regulate the activities of others!

The cardinal choice between markets and governments is also reflected in the no longer new "new federalism," a term invented in the Kennedy administration by Walter Heller and then given new life, though of uncertain duration, by the Reagan administration in 1981. The new federalism involves a review of the proper roles and responsibilities of federal, state, and local governments, as well as of the public and private sectors. This review relates, in a larger sense, to the cardinal issue of markets versus governments. The possible devolution of responsibility that is implicit in the idea of the new federalism carries with it the further implication that responsibilities initially devolved upon lower levels of government might, instead or subsequently, be assigned to the market, or to organizations that are neither market nor government organizations.[7] For example, nonprofit foundations might undertake manpower retraining, or provide various forms of social welfare services funded with private giving, as an alternative to government programs.

This cardinal issue is not only of central concern to the United States. It also impinges on Western Europe, on the Third World, on the remnants of the Second (Communist) World (notably China), and on the countries of Eastern Europe and the former Soviet Union that are seeking to transform their economies from centrally planned command systems to market-oriented ones. In Western Europe and Japan, the past three decades have seen a sustained growth in the role of government and a corresponding diminution in that of markets. For example, between 1960 and 1989, government spending in the OECD (Organization for Economic Cooperation and Development) countries, as a share of gross domestic product, rose from 28 percent to 42 percent (if so-called off-budget expenditures are added, the 1989 share is over 50 percent); comparable budget expenditure shares for the United States are 27 percent and 36 percent.[8] That the issue remains timely and active is reflected by the intensified efforts of the mixed conservative-socialist governments in France to denationalize state-owned industries and banks, open the state-owned television industry to competition by private television stations, and invoke market standards for determining industrial wage rates. Similarly, but less surprisingly, conservative governments in Britain have made strenuous efforts to denationalize state-owned industries and to reverse the growth of government as the dominant allocative agent in the economy. In Germany, the process of unifying the East German *länder* with West Germany has involved, since 1990, the use of government policy and resources to resurrect the role of the market and to privatize or liquidate the entire structure of formerly state-owned industry.

Even in China, which has a fundamental ideological commitment to resolving the allocation issue by centralized direction and government planning, rather than by markets and prices, its economic reform is a deliberate move in a similar direction: decentralization of economic decision making through market prices and competition in agriculture, in the small-scale consumer goods sector, and more extensively in China's several market-oriented "special economic zones," while centralized resource allocation prevails in the larger-scale industrial and infrastructure sectors. China's agricultural sector, while apparently decentralized, remains heavily influenced by large government subsidies as well as price controls.

And in Eastern Europe, Russia, Ukraine, and the other republics of the former Soviet Union, there is a pervasive commitment to marketization to replace their formerly government-dominated economies. Progress and prospects for implementing the several ingredients of effective marketization—notably, macroeconomic stabilization, price and wage decontrol, privatization and demonopolization, and currency convertibility—differ widely among these formerly centrally planned systems. But they all reflect a commitment to reach a new balance between markets and governments in which the market's determinative role will be expanded.

The same cardinal economic policy choice also arises in the multiple other worlds that we conveniently, if inaccurately, refer to as the Third World—inaccurately because this world is really not a single entity but rather multiple and heterogeneous groups of nations, whose diversity is in fact much greater than that within the other two worlds. Despite their diversity, most of these developing countries have thus far resolved the cardinal choice in favor of government control over major allocation decisions. The exceptions comprise a relatively small number of Third World countries including Hong Kong, Malaysia, Singapore, South Korea, Taiwan, and Turkey. These newly industrialized countries, despite occasional setbacks (partly as a result of occasional changes in their terms of trade, in the international price of oil, and in tightening of international capital markets), have by and large been the only successful instances of sustained economic growth in the Third World. And their success has been characterized by a relatively more prominent role played by market prices and competition, especially competition in international export markets, in resolving the cardinal economic policy choice. Since the late 1980s and early 1990s, several other developing countries—notably, Mexico, Indonesia, and Thailand—have been moving aggressively in the same direction. Generally, government policies in these countries have encouraged, rather than hindered, the market's active role. The Philippines, for a number of reasons peculiar to it, is a notable exception to this general picture: markets and price competition have been relatively active, yet Philippine economic performance in the past three decades has been dismal.

In most of the other 140 or so Third World countries, a strong statist, *dirigiste* disposition persists, mainly due to the historical association between socialism and the nationalist, anticolonialist movements of these countries. The state's predominant role in these economies has also been promoted by the benefits it conferred on those aspiring to, and eventually acquiring, power over the machinery of government. This statist legacy has waned in recent years as a result of accumulated evidence on the disappointing economic performance of centrally planned command economies in Cuba, Vietnam, Eastern Europe, and the former Soviet Union. Nevertheless, where the legacy remains, it contributes a pervasive influence tending to resolve the cardinal choice in favor of government rather than market allocationin favor of "theological" or "just" or "government-determined" prices, rather than market prices.[9]

The problem would be easier if the choice were between perfect markets and imperfect governments, or between perfect governments and imperfect markets. In fact, as already noted, the actual choice involves a compromise between imperfect markets and imperfect governments. This book seeks to illuminate that choice—if not a choice between evils, then at best between options that surely have flaws. More precisely, the purpose is to develop a theory of nonmarket failure so that the imperfect performance of governments can be analyzed with a clarity, and anticipated with a degree of accuracy, closer to that already reached in analyzing the imperfect performance of markets.

In contemplating the cardinal economic choice, we should consider the total effects associated with each of the options, rather than the shortcomings associated with only one.[10] We need to understand the more or less predictable shortcomings of governments no less than those of markets.

In this respect, politics has outpaced economics. Repeated electoral mandates by conservative governments in the United States, the United Kingdom, and Germany over the past decade reflect a widespread reaction in the political arena to the shortcomings of hyperactive governments, although there is some evidence that the political pendulum may reverse course in the 1990s. In any event, these reactions are due more to feelings and frustrations than to analysis and understanding. Without implying that analysis is more important than feelings in determining public policy, it does seem to me worthwhile to bring about a better balance between them. In the process, the content of formal economics can catch up to the realities of electoral politics. The relatively greater emphasis placed in this book on the shortcomings of governments arises from a judgment that modern economics, as well as the policies advocated by many economists and most other social scientists and policy analysts, has generally placed more analytic emphasis on the shortcomings of the market than on those of the nonmarket. Redressing one imbalance requires another.[11]

My emphasis on government failures does not imply that they are more or less egregious than those of the market. Rather, this emphasis derives from the belief that, whereas the failures of the market have already been fully expounded in logical and formal terms in the economics literature, those of the nonmarket have not been similarly analyzed.

Consequently, although the following pages make many references to market failures, they are purposely truncated by comparison with the more extensive exposition of nonmarket failures. The former is familiar because it has been treated fully elsewhere, while the latter—failure of the nonmarket—is not. I therefore have deliberately concentrated on the latter, rather than attempting to give equal treatment to both.

With this as the book's general motivation, chapter 2 reviews the existing theory of market failure and summarizes the generally familiar explanations of why market outcomes will predictably depart from both efficient and distributionally equitable outcomes, as well as why public perceptions of these failures may exaggerate the realities.

Chapter 3 begins to describe the theory of nonmarket failure, elaborating the inherent characteristics of the demand for and supply of government functions (i.e., the nonmarket sector) that account for the likely departure of nonmarket outcomes from efficient and distributionally equitable ones. An explanatory comment should be made about the method adopted in both chapters 3 and 4. That method involves an eclectic and inductive combination of anecdotes, data, and experience, on the one hand, and generalization and theory, on the other. In a technical sense, illustrations from government experience are cited to indicate the expected signs of the partial derivatives of nonmarket performance with respect to certain variables. For example, the exclusivity, or monopoly, that often is associated with nonmarket supply is likely to result in inflated or redundant costs—one of the several types of nonmarket failures.

Chapter 4 continues the exposition of nonmarket failure, with a typology of nonmarket failures that can be compared with that of market failure dealt with in chapter 2. Chapter 4 also considers the relative exposure of nonprofit organizations (NPOs) to the risks of nonmarket and market failure, suggesting that NPOs are usually more prone to the shortcomings of nonmarket than of market organizations.

Chapter 5, on implementation analysis, considers ways in which the theory of nonmarket failure can be drawn upon in the design, analysis, and evaluation of alternative public policies. Implementation analysis has two aims: first, to choose among policy alternatives on the basis of their proneness to nonmarket failure, or to reformulate them so they are less likely to go awry; and second, to build into the options eventually selected suitable means of avoiding or limiting the ensuing shortfalls. Thus, chapter 5 is less concerned with "why" and "what" than with "how to": that is, how to apply the theory and typology of nonmarket failure in designing improved public policies, and in comparing their respective strengths and shortcomings to those of market-oriented solutions.

Chapters 6 and 7 focus, respectively, on conceptual and empirical aspects of the comparison between market and nonmarket alternatives.

With respect to efficiency, chapter 6 adds to the criterion of allocative efficiency the criteria of dynamic efficiency, technological efficiency, and X-efficiency as important elements in comparing and choosing between market and nonmarket options. Chapter 6 also stresses the complexities introduced into the comparison by important noneconomic dimensions and criteria, including equity, participation, and accountability. Chapter 6 also reviews recent surveys of public attitudes toward the effectiveness of different levels of government.

Chapter 7 focuses on two different empirical approaches to efficiency comparisons between market and nonmarket systems: first, microefficiency, construed in terms of the relative costs of delivering homogeneous units of a specified product or service by private, market-oriented firms or by government agencies; and second, macroefficiency, construed in terms of the effects on real rates of economic growth of the relative size of the market and government (nonmarket) sectors in various countries.

The microefficiency comparisons review prior research on the relative performance of government and of the private sector in providing health services, public utilities, and various municipal services. The macroefficiency comparisons summarize some empirical work on the relation between the size of the government sector and the economic performance of developed and less-developed countries.

Chapter 8 presents conclusions and implications of the foregoing discussion. Chapter 8 suggests guidelines for choosing between markets and governments and discusses ways in which government can contribute to the improved functioning of markets and market forces can be utilized to improve the functioning of governments. The chapter also addresses the role of government in transforming command systems into market economies and concludes with observations on the respective dilemmas associated with market and nonmarket systems.

Notes

1. Of course, judgments about equity imply a prior choice of an appropriate yardstick. What is equitable according to one standard is not according to another (see the discussion of equity in chapter 4). Needless to say, Friedman and Galbraith use very different standards for judging equity.

2. For a fuller discussion of the theory of market failure, see chapter 2.

3. See Buchanan (1969), Buchanan and Tullock (1962), Niskanen (1971), and Forte and Peacock (1985).

4. For a full discussion of the theory of nonmarket failure, see chapters 3 and 4.

5. See especially Frederich von Hayek (1984). For a thorough analysis of the contributions of the "Austrian School" to markets-versus-governments issues, see DeBow (1991).

6. See Williamson (1985). For an earlier and similar view, see Arrow (1983).

7. It is worth noting that the older (1960s) and the newer (1980s) versions of new federalism differ in an important respect: the former was more disposed toward the devolution of certain federal government functions to a local or state level, whereas the "newer" new federalism is more disposed toward reassigning them to the market as well as to subsidiary levels of government.

8. See Organization for Economic Cooperation and Development (1991).

9. See Bauer (1984).

10. This purpose conforms closely to that of Coase's classic article (1960, 17ff., 42–44).

11. This general orientationcomparing markets and governments— is similar to that of C. E. Lindblom's *Politics and Markets* (1977), although the relative emphasis placed on government shortcomings (that is, nonmarket failures) is quite different from Lindblom's.

2   Market Failure

The Inadequacies of Markets

The principal justification for public policy intervention lies in the frequent and numerous shortcomings of market outcomes. Yet this rationale is only a necessary, not a sufficient, condition for policy formulation or for government intervention. The comment made a century ago by the British economist Henry Sidgwick can hardly be improved upon: "It does not follow that whenever laissez-faire falls short government interference is expedient; since the inevitable drawbacks of the latter may, in any particular case, be worse than the shortcomings of private enterprise."[1] Policy formulation properly requires that the realized shortcomings of market outcomes be compared with the potential shortcomings of nonmarket efforts to provide remedies. The pathology of market shortcomings or failures provides only limited help in prescribing therapies for government success.

But how is the success or failure of market outcomes to be judged? Two broad criteria are usually and properly, though sometimes ambiguously, employed: efficiency and distributional equity.

Market outcomes can be termed efficient if the same level of total benefits that they generate cannot be obtained at lower cost or, alternatively, if greater benefits cannot be generated at the same level of costs; in either case, the resulting total benefits must exceed total costs if the outcomes are to be deemed efficient. Efficiency is thus like a contest among different ways of doing a job: If the market can accomplish the job at a lower cost than can other institutional arrangements, or can do a better job for the same costs, then the market is relatively efficient. On the other hand, if other institutional arrangements can accomplish the task at lower cost, or can do it better for the same cost, then the market is, in this respect, relatively inefficient.

This criterion defines *allocative*, or *static*, *efficiency*. It can be extended and refined in various ways to allow for other types of efficiency. For example, *dynamic efficiency*—especially emphasized in the writings of Joseph Schumpeter—relates to the capability of free markets, or of other institutional arrangements, to promote new technology that lowers costs, improves product quality, or creates new and marketable products, and to promote these things at lower cost than other ways of doing them.[2] *X-efficiency*—a term coined by Harvey Leibenstein—relates to the capability of free markets or of other institutional arrangements to lower costs and raise the productivity of any given technology by stimulating organizational improvements, increased worker and management motivation, and improvements in a wide range of business decisions, including hiring and firing, promotions, salaries and bonuses, allocation of space, furniture, telephones, parking facilities, and so on.[3]

Whether markets are more or less able to promote these outcomes than are other institutional arrangements determines whether markets are relatively more or less dynamically efficient, or X-efficient, than are other institutional arrangements.

Although invoking the second criterion for judging market outcomesdistributional equity—goes beyond the conventional boundaries of microeconomics, this criterion has profound significance for formulating, evaluating, and implementing alternative public policies. Economists are less comfortable in grappling with the murkiness of distributional issues than with the relative precision of efficiency issues. Yet the treatment of tax incidence, for example, is central to the field of public finance, and tax incidence is quintessentially distributional in character. However, even in this instance, economists usually evaluate alternative redistributive and tax programs from the standpoint of minimizing their negative effects on economic efficiency. In the real world of public policy—whether pertaining to education, energy, housing, foreign trade, or even defense policy—distributional issues are usually more influential than efficiency ones in shaping judgments about the success or shortcomings of market outcomes. As Jacob Viner observed, extensive government intervention in the free market has come about ". . . largely as the result of dissatisfaction with the prevailing distribution of income. . . . No modern people will have zeal for the free market unless it operates in a setting of 'distributive justice' with which they are tolerably content."[4]

Even when the central importance of distributional equity is acknowledged, the question remains, What standard should be used to evaluate it? The answer will be very different, and often ambiguous, depending on whether equity is interpreted in the sense of equality of outcome or equality of opportunity, or in the sense of horizontal equity or vertical equity, or in the Marxian sense, or in the sense of the Old Testament or the New Testament, or in the sense of assuring that the least-favored have their lot improved before any further improvements are allowed for those who are more favored.[5]

That markets may fail to produce either economically optimal (efficient) or socially desirable (equitable) outcomes has been elaborated in a well-known and voluminous literature.[6] Although the last word on this subject has not been written, the essential points in the accepted theory of market failure are worth summarizing as background for the subsequent discussion of nonmarket failure.[7]

Types of Market Failure

There are four sources or types of market shortcomings or failures. I use the terms *shortcomings* and *failures* interchangeably; strictly speaking, shortcomings has a looser and more inclusive meaning. Most economists would confine market failure to departures from Pareto-efficient outcomes, thereby excluding distributional issues except to the extent that distribution affects efficiency. By contrast, many noneconomists (and even some economists) argue that distribution has, or should have, priority over efficiency, and they fault the market precisely because of its failure to accord this priority.[8] The choice between disciplinary orthodoxy and practical relevance seems clear to me. This book therefore regards distributional considerations as lying within the purview of market shortcomings or failures.

Externalities and Public Goods

Where economic activities create spillovers, whether benefits or costs, that are not, respectively, appropriable by or collectible from the producer, then market outcomes will not be efficient in the allocative sense defined previously. Since these external benefits or costs do not enter the calculations upon which production decisions are based, too little will tend to be produced where the externalities are (net) benefits, and too much where they are (net) costs, compared with socially efficient output levels. Education is an example of an activity that putatively yields positive externalities (benefits) for society at large in addition to the benefits directly derived by the recipient. These externalities provide a rationale for government intervention—through subsidy or direct public sector production or regulation—to compensate for the tendency of the market, if it is not prodded, to produce insufficient output. Other instances of positive externalities are the knowledge and technology resulting from activities and expenditures devoted to research and development. To the extent these benefits are external to, and nonappropriable by, the firms that bear the associated costs, these and other firms will invest too little in R&D. Once again, the market will fail according to the criterion of allocative efficiency unless government intervenes by subsidizing or otherwise stimulating these activities. Moreover, to the extent that dynamic efficiency—the development of new products and processes—also depends on the creation of knowledge and technology, the unfettered market will fall short on this criterion as well.

Chemical and noise emissions from aircraft or other industrial activities are examples of negative externalities (costs). Their existence provides a rationale for government intervention—through taxing or direct regulation—to compensate for the market's tendency to produce excessive output in this instance, because the externalities are otherwise not taken into account.

Private goods that are associated with externalities can be distinguished from *public goods:* the former term applies where *most* of the benefits or costs associated with output are, respectively, collected or paid by the producer, although *some* are not; and the latter (public goods) applies where most of an activity's consequences consist of nonappropriable benefits (for example, national security, which is the classic example of a genuinely public good) or noncollectible costs (for example, crime, the classic public "bad").

A distinction can be made between the nonappropriable consequences (benefits or costs) associated with externalities and the joint or collective consumption associated with public goods. In the latter case, the consequences are enjoyed by or imposed on all; hence, nonappropriability is implicit in public goods.

However, the notion of public goods can also be viewed as the limiting case of a private good with overwhelmingly large externalities. The water pollution associated with some chemical processing plants illustrates this latter case. Viewed in this light, externalities are a more general concept than public goods.[9]

A powerful counterargument to the market failure created by externalities was made by Ronald Coase (1960). Coase contends that externalities do not necessarily lead to market failure, provided that a transaction or contract can be struck between the source and recipients that, in effect, brings the externalities into the market.[10] He argues that those who are the victims of external costs (such as the external costs imposed by chemical or noise emissions) can make these costs tangible to their sources by offering to pay the latter to desist or diminish the culpable activities (for example, to refrain from or reduce the emissions). Once the offer has been made, continuance of the emissions becomes a tangible cost, because the perpetrator will lose the offered payment unless he refrains from the objectionable activity. Consequently, in an effort to eat his cake and have it, a rational, cool, and calculating source of such negative externalities will seek to diminish them. Toward this end, the source will consider, for example, using different chemical processes, or following different routes, or developing appropriate new technology enabling it to continue its production activities (which accounted for the emissions in the first place), without incurring the costs that have been made tangible by the victims' offer.

Unfortunately, Coase's powerful theoretical argument runs into a serious problem of implementation. The problem lies in the difficulty of bringing about the kind of bargain or contract he envisages between the sources and the victims of the negative externalities.[11] In practice, the difficulty (which implies costs) of accomplishing such transactions between perpetrators and victims, or between benefactors and beneficiaries, may be so formidable as to preclude the bargain being struck at all. However, to the extent these formidable transaction costs can be avoided or surmounted, markets can overcome externalities and continue to function efficiently. In that event, the distribution of benefits that results from the adjusted, and now once-more efficient, market outcomes will be altered. Under the assumed bargain, the beneficiary or the victim of the prior externalities will have to part with some income in order to avoid the negative externalities or retain the positive ones, respectively. Thus, the efficiency of market outcomes will be preserved, while its distributional equity may be enhanced or diminished, depending on the equity criterion that is applied (see the discussion that follows on distributional equity).

Increasing Returns

Where economic activities are subject to increasing returns and decreasing marginal costs, markets will again fail to generate efficient outcomes. Under conditions of decreasing costs, the lowest cost mode of production would be achieved by a single producer. Consequently, a free market will result in monopoly. Assuming that the monopolist cannot discriminate in the prices charged to different buyers, and hence a single price prevails in the market (single-part pricing), the outcome will be inefficient, in both static and dynamic terms. In static terms, the outcome will be inefficient because the quantity produced will be lower, and the profit-maximizing price charged by the monopolist will be higher, than warranted by the costs of production. In terms of dynamic efficiency, as defined earlier, the outcome will also leave something to be desired because incentives for innovation by a secure and unchallenged monopolist will be weaker than would likely prevail under a more competitive regime.

Where increasing returns exist, various types of government intervention may be justified to alter the market outcome: (1) through direct operation or regulation of a "natural" monopoly (for example, public utilities), by setting prices or allowable rates of return on its capital, at levels closer to those that would prevail in a competitive environment; (2) through legal protection to prevent a single-firm takeover and to encourage competition (for example, through antitrust legislation). Such types of intervention depart from a theoretically efficient outcome, although they seek to approach it.[12]

A recent development in economics—the theory of contestable markets—suggests that, even in the face of increasing returns and the prevalence of monopoly, strong tendencies may persist for efficient, or nearly efficient, pricing and output decisions by monopolists, thereby avoiding or mitigating the impact of this source of market failure. The theory of contestable markets has been developed by William Baumol, and was foreshadowed several decades ago by the French economist François Perroux. Perroux suggested that, if markets are open to new entrants and there are few barriers and limited costs to entry, monopolists will be disciplined by the potential entry of competitors (the "potential rival"), who would contest the monopolized market unless profit margins are kept low and output is kept high.[13]

Thus, where barriers to entry are low, the production of a good or provision of a service by a monopolist does not necessarily signify that it will be able to exploit monopoly power. In the case of the airline industry, for example, even monopoly suppliers of service on thinly served routes have been unable to charge monopoly prices because the existence of potential entrants and competitors has discouraged such practices by the existing monopolists. Consequently, following deregulation of the airlines, rates charged on thinly served routes have not been characterized by monopoly pricing or monopoly profits any more than have the heavily served and clearly competitive routes.[14]

Even for the Schumpeterian criterion of dynamic efficiency, increasing returns and monopolistic market structure may not stray as far from the desirable goal of innovation and rising productivity as has usually been assumed. Here again the influence of the contestability of the market by potential entrants (rivals) may enforce a strong discipline on monopolists, obliging them to maintain a high level of R&D and to sustain rapid innovation to protect their presently monopolized markets. Potential competition may thus have an effect similar to that of actual competition.

The breakup of AT&T, after lengthy litigation in which the huge corporation was found in violation of antitrust legislation, provides an interesting example of the conflict between the two preceding types of market failure: externalities and increasing returns. To remedy one source of market failure (increasing returns), the courts have perhaps created another (externalities). Perceiving a lack of effective competition in an industry subject to increasing returns (telecommunications), the courts have replaced it by a situation in which benefits from undertaking R&D and innovation, which formerly were largely internalized by the giant AT&T, are now largely external to the seven or eight regional firms into which the industry has been split. Hence, incentives may be weakened for the newly competing entities in the telecommunications industry to undertake as aggressive efforts in R&D and technological improvement as did AT&T in the past. The disincentives arise because of the externalities that R&D generates: Competitors can free ride on the R&D expenses incurred by any one firm. By contrast, when AT&T dominated the entire market, the results of R&D and innovation were internalized by the single firm that benefited from, as well as generated, them. Hence, the free rider problem was avoided.

At the same time, the breakup of AT&T may spur technological efficiency and X-efficiency as each of the new regional firms competes with the others to capture larger market shares. So, on the one hand, the breakup decision may stimulate technological advancement by enhancing competition; yet, on the other hand, the same decision may diminish such advancement because of the externalities and free rider problems that ensue and that may reduce incentives for R&D and technological innovation.

The AT&T case illustrates a frequent experience in the public policy arena. Public policy efforts motivated by the aim of remedying one type of shortcoming may well create a different one as a by-product. It remains to be seen how the balance of advantage between these two sources of market failure—externalities and increasing returns—will work out under the altered market structure established in the telecommunications industry.

Market Imperfections

Where the price, information, and mobility characteristics of perfect markets depart significantly from those prevailing in actual markets, the outcomes resulting from those markets will not be efficient. Once again, a rationale arises for government intervention. Where prices and interest rates, for one reason or another, do not indicate relative scarcities and opportunity costs, where consumers do not have equal access to information about products and markets, where information about market opportunities and production technology is not equally available to all producers, or where factors of production are restricted in their ability to move in response to such information, market forces will not allocate efficiently and the economy will produce below its capacity. These conditions abound in the economies of less developed countries, and they are surely not unfamiliar in the economies of more developed ones. Indeed, these imperfections apply to some extent in all markets and to a great extent in some. In such circumstances, the implication for public policy is to reduce, if not remove, these imperfections: to facilitate availability of information, to lower barriers to entry and mobility, and so on.[15]

However, where many of the conditions required for efficient functioning of markets do not exist, improving some will not necessarily improve the efficiency of the market as a whole. Consequently, the policy implications of market imperfections may be ambiguous.[16] Legal protection of patents provides an example of how one type of market imperfection may even contribute to market efficiency. In this case the market imperfection is the restriction of access to technological information that is created by patents. A short-run loss of efficiency results because firms that do not hold the patent are restricted in their access to improved technological information because of the price (royalty) they have to pay to obtain and to use it. Consumers are thus deprived of benefits in the short run. However, the purpose of the patent restriction is to enhance incentives for technological improvement, thereby contributing to dynamic efficiency in the long run. The presumption is that the long-run gains, due to enhancement of incentives and the resulting impetus to dynamic efficiency, will exceed the short-term losses resulting from diminished allocative efficiency.

In less developed countries, the scale and pervasiveness of market imperfections—and sometimes even the apparent absence of functioning markets—is often adduced as a rationale for government dominance and control in the economy. A "big push" by government is presumed to be needed to compensate for the inadequacies of markets.

Certainly, market imperfections abound in these countries. They are characterized by restricted access to economically relevant information, factor immobilities, price and interest rate distortions, and so on. Yet despite these characteristics, it is a striking fact that the few relatively successful developing countries—Hong Kong, Malaysia, Singapore, South Korea, and Taiwan—have greatly benefited from decisions and policies that limit the government's role in economic decision making, and instead allow markets—notwithstanding their imperfections and shortcomings—to exercise a major role in determining resource allocations.[17]

Distributional Equity

As already noted, most economists exclude distributional effects from judgments about the success or failure of markets. In textbook usage, the term *market failure* is usually confined to departures from competitive equilibrium and strictly efficient (Pareto-efficient) outcomes; as narrowly construed, then, market failure typically excludes departures from distributional equity. Nevertheless, this exclusion is usually accompanied by an acknowledgment that the distributional results of even well-functioning markets may not accord with socially accepted standards of equity, or with society's preferences for reducing excessive disparities in the distribution of income and wealth. It is also usually acknowledged that, where there is a trade-off between efficiency and equity, social consensus in democratic systems often is prepared to forgo some of the one to realize more of the other.[18] In welfare economics this trade-off is usually dealt with by considering the relative efficiency of various redistributive measures (for example, income taxes, excises, subsidies, unemployment relief, and income transfers) in achieving a desired redistribution (that is, minimizing the allocative distortions resulting from the income and substitution effects of redistribution).

Nevertheless, from one perspective, it is theoretically correct to consider distributional inequity as an example of market failure. From this perspective, income distribution is a particular type of public good. An equitable redistribution does not result from freely functioning markets because philanthropy and charity yield benefits that are external to, and not appropriable by, the donors, but are instead realized by society as a whole. Left to its own devices, the market will therefore produce less redistribution than is efficient (that is, socially desirable), because of the usual free rider problem associated with externalities, public goods, and incomplete markets.[19] Another perspective for viewing distributional equity is quite unrelated to market failure in the strict sense. From this perspective, the equilibrium redistribution mentioned above may be quite inequitable in terms of one or another ethical norm. Even if the market could surmount the narrow type of failure described earlier, its distributional outcome might still be socially and ethically unacceptable from the standpoint of one or more such norms.[20] On these grounds, the distributional outcomes of even perfectly functioning markets can be justifiably criticized.

As noted earlier, Jacob Viner pointed out several decades ago that the decisive test of the acceptability of markets in modern democratic societies depends fundamentally on the extent to which such markets can coexist within a general setting of "distributive justice" with which the electorate is "tolerably content."[21] Furthermore, most public policy decisions are usually even more concerned with distributional issues (namely, *who* gets the benefits and *who* pays the costs) than with efficiency issues (namely, how *large* are the benefits and costs). Since the principal aim of this book is to compare market shortcomings with the shortcomings of nonmarket remedies, distributional inequity will be included among the offenses.

Notes

1. See Sidgwick (1887, 414) and Cairncross (1976).

2. See, for example, Schumpeter (1934).

3. Leibenstein (1966).

4. See Viner (1960, 68).

5. See chapter 4 for a more extensive discussion of these several standards of equity.

6. See, for example, Reder (1947), Samuelson (1954), Lipsey and Lancaster (1956), Little (1957), Bator (1958), Musgrave (1959), Viner (1960, 45–69), Mishan (1969), Arrow (1971), Rawls (1971), Davis and Hewlett (1977), Thurow (1981, 183–193), and Tew, Broder, and Musser (1982, 1091).

7. As Arrow (1971) observes, "The clarification of these concepts [relating to market failure] is a long, historical process, not yet concluded."

8. See, for example, Rawls's "second principle" of a just society (Rawls, 1971).

9. Private benefits approach zero, and all remaining benefits are external. More precisely, if v_{ij}^s is the valuation placed, or the price paid, by the ith person for the jth unit of a good s, and mc_j^s is its marginal cost of production, then the condition for an allocatively efficient level of output for a private good with externalities is

$$mc_j^s = v_{ij}^s + \sum_{m=1}^{k} v_{mj}^s$$

where v_{ij} is the price paid by i and the $\sum v^s_{mj}$ are externalities (experienced by all other k individuals as a result of i's consumption of the jth unit of s), positive if the externalities are benefits and negative if costs. The v^s_{mj} indicate what each of the k individuals would, in principle, be willing to pay to receive (or avoid) the jth unit. However, if the k individuals realize the benefits or costs whether or not they pay for them, then the latter are nonappropriable, and consumption is collective.

For a "pure" public good, $v^s_{ij} = 0$. Consumption is entirely collective, and no single unit is purchased by anybody. The optimum condition then is:

$$mc^s_j = \sum_{m=1}^{k} v^s_{mj}$$

Compare Mishan (1969). This condition is sometimes misstated as equivalent to a zero marginal cost of production. For example, the marginal cost of national defense in, say, the United States or NATO is *not* zero, although nontaxpayers, as well as citizens of other countries, receive the resulting benefits. The generalized explanation for the existence of externalities and public goods is that markets do not exist for capturing some benefits or levying some costs. Nonexistence of markets in these cases is explained by (1) the high cost or inability of excluding beneficiaries (for example, from the benefits of national defense or police expenditures), or of establishing property rights as a basis for claiming liability when they are infringed (for example, noise emissions in airport vicinities); and (2) the lack of information required for market transactions to be concluded (for example, ascertaining what the "true" v_{ij} are in the previous discussion), due at least in part to the free rider problem associated with (1).

10. See Coase (1960). Coase's identification of the central importance of transaction costs led to Williamson's development of "transaction cost economics." See Williamson (1985).

11. It should be clear that Coase's line of argument can be applied to positive externalities (external benefits) as well as to negative externalities. In this case, the potential bargain would be one in which the source of the external benefits would try to extract a payment by threatening to eliminate or reduce the benefits unless the beneficiaries compensate him for these windfalls. However, credibility of the threat may be impaired because the responsible

source would very likely have to incur costs to carry it out: the beneficiaries must be persuaded that the threatener just might be willing to deprive himself of some gains in pursuit of larger ones.

12. Some discussions of market failure include increasing returns (for example, Bator, 1958), while others exclude it. Arrow, for example, contrasts increasing returns ("essentially a technological phenomenon") with market failure (which relates to "the mode of economic organization" (Arrow, 1971). I think this categorization leaves something to be desired. For example, improvements in technology can eliminate or at least reduce externalities (which Arrow considers market failures because they relate to the "mode of economic organization") by resolving the problems of exclusion and nonappropriability. As an illustration, electronic warning and protection devices may be an efficient means of lowering the risk of theft for households purchasing them. One can also imagine acoustical and air-filtration devices that would reduce the negative externalities represented by airport emissions or identify their source as a basis for imposing and collecting costs. Conversely, Arrow's "technological" phenomenon of increasing returns can be reconciled with efficient pricing and output by suitable modes of economic organization, for example, through multipart pricing. (For a discussion of various pricing and market devices for reconciling increasing returns with efficient operation, see Wolf et al., 1975). Increasing returns are a source of market inefficiency only as long as markets do not exist for *separate* units of the same good. Allowing for enough subscripting, in the Arrow-Debreu sense, and hence separability of commodities, increasing returns are theoretically as compatible with competitive equilibrium as are externalities.

13. See Baumol, Panzar, and Willig (1982) and Perroux (1957, 18).

14. Federal Reserve Bank of San Francisco (1984, 2).

15. See the discussion in chapter 8 of opportunities for government actions designed to improve the functioning of markets.

16. This is the essential message of second-best theory (Lipsey and Lancaster, 1956). For example, changing a tariff that has applied equally to imports from all countries so that it applies instead only to a few countries may reduce efficiency. Trade will be diverted as well as created, and the loss from the former may exceed the gains from the latter (see Viner, 1950).

17. See Wolf (1981a).

18. Little (1957). See also Scitovsky (1951) and Okun (1975).

19. The point can be formulated more precisely. Individual demands for redistribution can be defined in the same notional sense in which such demands can be defined for defense, or for law and order. For example, the demand for redistribution can be expressed as the desired *change* in current distribution (as measured, say, by the Gini coefficient); demand for redistribution is presumed to decline as the desired amount of voluntary individual philanthropy per dollar of earned income rises. Presumably, individual willingness to pay for redistribution declines as the price of achieving it rises. A cost function for redistribution can also be defined in terms of the same two variables. In principle, individual demands could be added, and the social equilibrium level of redistribution would be that for which the marginal optimization condition is satisfied (see note 9). This equilibrium redistribution is not achieved because there is either no market or an incomplete market for philanthropy, just as there is an incomplete market for defense. In both cases, voluntary donations (unless motivated by special tax incentives) would be lacking due to the usual nonappropriability and nonexcludability reasons.

20. See the preceding discussion concerning the different standards of equity and the more extended discussion in chapter 4.

21. See Viner (1960, 68).

3

Nonmarket Failure: The Demand and Supply Conditions

Market Failure and Government Intervention

The shortcomings of the market described in chapter 2 provide the most convincing rationale for attempts by government (that is, the nonmarket) to remedy them. This rationale can be influential even if political actors and decision makers are unaware of both the terminology and the theory of market failure. They simply perceive that operation of the market fails to accomplish something regarded as wholesome, desirable, or otherwise appropriate. Hence, government intervention may be advocated to remedy the perceived miscarriage. Whether these perceptions are valid or mistaken will not affect the advocacy, although their validity may be important to others who remain to be convinced. I shall return later to consider how public perceptions of the market's failures may be shaped in ways that distort, at least in the short run, the demand for nonmarket remedies.

The theory of market failure (including its distributional component) is sufficiently elastic to support particular regulatory interventions designed (by a lobbyist, or a legislator, or the executive branch) to favor a particular constituent. For example, price supports for agricultural output, as well as other forms of farm subsidies, have been justified on the grounds that normal market prices fail to allow for the collective social benefits of preserving a healthy rural sector in the economy. Similarly, advocacy of substantial government support for scientific and technological research is based on the argument that such research yields external benefits that cannot be appropriated by those who are responsible for generating them. And public support for both education and health care proceeds from the presumption that these services are associated with various externalities, including distributional equity as well as moral, social, and ethical benefits for the community at large, above and beyond the benefits of those directly receiving the services.

An extension of this line of argument has led to advocacy and enactment of "voluntary" quotas to limit U.S. imports of automobiles and steel—a policy that is justified on grounds of social fairness and the collective importance of these industries for the security and well-being of the country as a whole. (The result has been a hidden tax on consumers, and temporarily high windfall profits in the automobile industry followed, not surprisingly, by continued erosion of its competitive position in international as well as domestic markets.)

The public choice paradigm of government behavior explains these occurrences as the result of formal collusion or informal collaboration between potentially benefiting constituencies (for example, the farm lobby, the science and technology community, the health and education lobbies, and the automobile and steel industries) and the cognizant government agencies and congressional committees.[1] In some instances, a line can be clearly drawn between the public choice explanation for preferential treatment and the public good justification. The public good argument focuses on the broad social justification for action that happens, incidentally, to favor a particular group (for example, affirmative action advocacy by the NAACP, or advocacy of protection for the steel industry or of the merchant marine on national security grounds); the public choice position focuses instead on the motivation provided by the self-serving character of the preferential action itself, treating any attempts at broad social justification as disingenuous and contrived (import quotas and agricultural price supports are examples).

Yet the line between the two arguments is often blurred. Protecting American auto producers averts or alleviates serious hardship to families of auto workers who would be unemployed if Japanese cars (allegedly helped by unfair advantages from tax benefits and other subsidies) had full access to the U.S. market. Thus, the failure of the market to yield distributional outcomes deemed by the political process to be fair, or at least acceptable, may lead to preferential treatment favoring a particular group (for example, subsidies for farmers). From the standpoint of public good arguments, this is an instance of market failure—albeit one that stretches credibility. However, from the standpoint of the public choice argument, such preferment represents a failure or shortcoming of the *nonmarket*—that is, a miscarriage of public policy: society as a whole is demonstrably worse off, because the benefits realized by the favored group are less than the total costs imposed on the rest of society. We shall return to this dimension of nonmarket failure later.

Thus, the market's distributional shortcomings, as well as its actual or potential efficiency shortcomings, often lead to effective demands for nonmarket intervention to bring about more equitable or more efficient outcomes. That these intended results often do not ensue is explained by the theory of nonmarket failure.

The Nonmarket: Demand and Supply Characteristics

The basis for distinguishing between the market and the nonmarket is that market organizations derive their principal revenues from prices charged for output sold in markets where buyers can choose what to buy as well as whether to buy, whereas nonmarket organizations derive their principal revenues from taxes, donations, or other nonpriced sources. Although government is clearly the largest and most influential component, the nonmarket sector also includes foundations, state-supported universities, churches, PTAs, and the Boy Scouts. The typology of nonmarket failure developed here applies principally to the performance shortfalls of government but encompasses those associated with other nonmarket organizations as well. As discussed earlier, the absence of perfect and complete markets accounts for the various types of market failure. Similarly, nonmarket failures are due to the absence of nonmarket mechanisms for reconciling calculations by decision makers of their private and organizational costs and benefits with the costs and benefits of society as a whole. Nor, for reasons we shall suggest later, are prospects for the invention of suitable nonmarket mechanisms that will avoid nonmarket failure notably brighter than for creating and perfecting suitable markets whose absence leads to market failures. In other words, where the market's "hidden hand" does not turn "private vices into public virtues," it may be no less difficult to construct visible nonmarket hands that will turn public vices into public virtues.

Public policies intended to compensate for market shortcomings generally take the form of legislative or administrative assignment of particular functions to one or another government agency to produce specified outputs that are expected to redress the market's shortcomings. These outputs or activities are of four types: (1) regulatory services (for example, environmental regulation, radio and television licensing, interstate commerce regulation, food and drug control); (2) "pure" public goods (national defense, space research and development); (3) quasi-public goods (education, postal services, health research); and (4) administering transfer payments (federal, state, and local welfare programs, social security, etc.). The value of these outputs is expressed in national accounts as exactly equal to the cost of the inputs used in producing them. But this accounting convenience implies nothing about the efficiency or the social or economic value of the activities themselves. Nor does it explain the reasons why these outputs and activities are likely to result in specific types of nonmarket failure. This explanation lies in the special demand and supply characteristics that, in degree or in kind, distinguish such nonmarket activities and outputs from those of the market. These distinguishing characteristics can be used to define nonmarket demands and supplies, and these in turn result in particular types of failures or shortcomings to which nonmarket activities are prone.

The Conditions of Nonmarket Demand

The conditions of demand may contribute to shortcomings in the delivery of government (i.e., nonmarket) services by inflating the demand for such services. Some of these conditions have grown stronger over time, while others are perennial. These demand conditions can be summarized under five headings.

1. Increased public awareness of market shortcomings

In recent decades, especially in the period from the 1930s to 1980, a dramatic increase occurred in public awareness of the shortcomings of the market. This change was due both to the acknowledged failures of market outcomes to be socially optimal (e.g., the growth of toxic wastes and pollutants, the visible exercise of monopoly power by both business and labor, increased population density and its effect on congestion and, hence, on the generally greater importance of externalities) and to wider dissemination of information about these lapses. Instances of market failure have increased in frequency and in magnitude as economic activity has expanded. Such failures have also been the subject of vigorous and expanded activity by the information media, as well as by environmental groups and consumer organizations, to publicize these shortcomings. Increased public awareness of these shortcomings has understandably led to reduced tolerance of them.

2. Political organization and enfranchisement

The increase in actual market failures, and in public awareness of them, has been reflected in and influenced by the organization and political enfranchisement of many groups and interests that formerly were less informed and less active in the political process, for example, women's groups, minorities, student groups, environmentalists, consumer groups, and nuclear power advocates and their opponents. And these groups have, especially in the 1960s and 1970s, pressed for governmental legislation, regulation, and other programs to remedy the failures of the market to produce outcomes desired by their advocates. Class action suits, contingent lawyers' fees, and judicial rulings and claims awards have provided additional impetus for nonmarket interventions to redress market shortcomings.

3. The structure of political rewards

In the political process, which mediates these heightened public demands for remedial government action, rewards often accrue to legislators and governmental officials who articulate and publicize problems and legislate proposed solutions, without assuming responsibility for implementing them.

4. The high time-discount of political actors

In part as a consequence of this reward structure, and of the short terms associated with elected office, the rate of time-discount of political actors may be higher than that of society. The result is often an appreciable disjuncture between the short time horizons of political actors and the longer time required to analyze, experiment with, and understand a particular problem or market shortcoming, in order to see whether a practical remedy exists at all. Hence, future costs and future benefits tend to be heavily discounted or ignored, while current or near-term benefits and costs are magnified. The result is what Feldstein has called "the inherent myopia of the political process."[2]

A dramatic example of such myopia is provided by the pervasive growth in the 1960s and 1970s of large-scale redistributive social welfare programs in the United States and Western Europe, generously protected and boosted by automatic cost-of-living adjustments. Enactment of these programs was galvanized by a widespread disposition among legislators and executives in the Western democracies to overestimate the short-term benefits (perhaps especially the political benefits) of these programs and to underestimate their long-term costs. This myopia was reflected in the failure to realize in the 1960s that Medicare and Medicaid, designed to help the elderly and the poor, would lead to an explosion in health care costs and an enormous increase in the share of the gross national product absorbed by the health sector—from 5.3 percent in 1960 to 10.8 percent in 1983 and to 12.2 percent in 1990.[3] It was similarly reflected in a failure to realize that expanded welfare programs, such as Aid for Families with Dependent Children, although intended to provide help for poor families, might have the effect of seriously weakening the structure of the family.[4]

5. Decoupling between burdens and benefits
Finally, a distortion of nonmarket demand often arises from the decoupling between those who receive the

benefits, and those who pay the costs, of government programs.[5] The classic free rider problem is a special case of decoupling: benefits are extended to all, or to specified groups, regardless of whether any particular member pays. Where benefits and costs are borne by different groups, incentives toward political organization and lobbying by prospective beneficiaries predictably lead to demands that may be both politically effective and economically inefficient. Examples are provided by agricultural price supports and subsidies in both the American and Western European economies, as well as other forms of protection for particular interests and sectors: tariffs; voluntary and mandatory import quotas; concessional loans and export credits to foreign countries to stimulate exports by the lending countries.

This decoupling between beneficiaries and victims can explain the absence of government intervention as well as its presence. For example, in the case of gun control in the United States, prospective beneficiaries, namely, the public at large, are numerous and dispersed, while those who would incur the costs of control are concentrated and well organized, notably, the National Rifle Association. The incentives of the dispersed majority may be too weak to overcome the resistance of the concentrated minority. Even though the aggregate social benefits from gun control may exceed the costs that would be imposed on the gunners, control by government does not occur. The political process may not provide an effective means by which the public beneficiaries could offer compensation to the gun enthusiasts to induce them to relinquish guns or to accept restrictive licensing of them.

Two different aspects of this decoupling phenomenon are worth distinguishing. What might be called "microdecoupling" arises where the benefits from an existing or prospective government program are concentrated in a particular group, while the costs are broadly dispersed among the public, as taxpayers or consumers. The beneficiaries thus have stronger incentives, and may make politically more effective efforts, to initiate, sustain, or expand a particular program than the victims have, or make, to oppose it. The result may be a government program or regulation that is inefficient (aggregate costs exceed benefits), or inequitable, or both.

Examples include agricultural price supports in the United States mentioned earlier, the Common Agricultural Policy of the European Common Market, and those increases in Social Security benefits over the past three decades that have made the income of retirees more fully protected against inflation than that of most of the employed, tax-paying labor force.

The second type of decoupling—"macrodecoupling"—constitutes a fundamental and inherent problem of demand for government programs in Western democracies. Macrodecoupling is quintessentially a problem of political economy, rather than of economics. It is also a source of inefficiency over time, rather than at a particular point in time. Macrodecoupling arises because political power rests with the voting majority, while a minority provides most of the tax base. The result is an opportunity and incentive to expand redistributive programs since the "demand" depends on the majority, while the supply of revenues comes from the minority. Whereas microdecoupling implies that a well-organized minority can exploit the majority, macrodecoupling implies that the majority can exploit the minority.

The result of macrodecoupling, in the absence of restraint by the majority, can be erosion of the mainsprings of investment, innovation, and growth, if the lower-income majority's temptation to redistribute before-tax income weakens the upper income minority's incentive to invest and innovate. It may be equally true that, unless the upper-income

minority's affluence and the resulting distributional disparities are restrained, social disharmony, resentment, and an-
tagonism will not be!

The enormous expansion of entitlement and other social
programs in the United States (and in Western Europe) since
the mid-1960s is, to some extent, a reflection of this decoupling: student loans and scholarships; subsidized housing
programs for low-income families; Medicaid and Medicare;
food stamps and legal aid to indigents; disability insurance;
comprehensive employment and training programs; urban
transit; etc. The results of this expansion have been extraordinary. In 1980, 36 million Americans received monthly
Social Security checks. Benefits were received by 22 million
from Medicaid, 28 million from Medicare, 18 million from
food stamps, 15 million from Veterans' programs, and 11
million from Aid for Families with Dependent Children
(AFDC).[6] By 1992, these numbers had risen still further:
Social Security 44 million, Medicaid 36 million, Medicare 30
million, food stamps 26 million, AFDC 14 million.[7] Feldstein
cites an estimate that perhaps half of the U.S. population
depends in whole or in part on federal aid in one form or
another![8]

Both types of decoupling may contribute to "excess" demand for government activities (programs, regulations, redistribution)—excess either in the sense that they entail
greater social costs than benefits, or that they are not sus-
tainable because they diminish incentives for productivity
and growth in the economy.

That many of the conditions discussed above may result
in distortions of nonmarket demand does not imply that all
increases in nonmarket demand represent distortions. For
example, nonmarket demand may be expected to rise with
real income. To the extent that nonmarket goods are "supe-
rior" goods—that is, goods with a high income elasticity of
demand (for example, parks, museums, public recreational

facilities)—their demand will rise more than in proportion to income growth. To the extent that expanded education, as well as real income, results in greater empathy for the needy, government transfer programs may also be expected to grow.

Nevertheless, conditions of demand in Western democracies can often lead to profound distortions in politically effective demands for government action or inaction. The principal culprits are (1) the often excessively high time-discounts of elected officials, resulting from the relentless pressure of the relatively short intervals between election campaigns; and (2) the decoupling between those who benefit from, and those who pay for, government programs, frequently resulting in stronger incentives to expand than to confine government programs. As a result, government programs may be initiated or expanded even though they are inefficient in a microeconomic sense (e.g., tariffs, agricultural price supports), as well as inequitable in conferring special gains and privileges on politically effective groups, while imposing greater costs on politically less effective ones. Other programs may be expanded to a level where they become inefficient in a dynamic sense (e.g., entitlement programs) by undermining the incentives on which the economy's longer-term growth depends.

Perceptions and the Demand for Nonmarket Activities

The demand characteristics previously described relate to public perceptions of the inadequacies and shortcomings of market outcomes. The correspondence between these perceptions and the realities of market failure, including distributional failure, may or may not be close. As the British philosopher Coddington has observed, perceptions do not represent knowledge, or even "knowledge deficiencies," but rather "knowledge surrogates." Such surrogates are more analogous to conjecture, wishes, or fears than to reality, or even to genuine uncertainty about the complex structure of reality.[9] Various influences can operate to distort perceptions and increase their remoteness from the "facts." For example, the incentives of the news media, political actors, and special interest groups often lead them to magnify newsworthy instances of actual market failure (e.g., collusion, restricted entry, corruption, pollution, monopolistic profits) and to highlight the frequent inequity of market outcomes, both in itself and as a major source of prevailing or potential (social) instability. Part of the distinction arises simply because problems, shortcomings, and miscarriages are intrinsically more dramatic and eye-catching than is satisfactory, or even successful, performance. Bylines are more often captured by dramatizing a disquieting event than by placing it in a balanced perspective. A second element contributing to distortion probably lies in the self-selection bias that animates publicists. A far larger proportion of their members than of other professional groups, or of the public at large, tends to be critical, if not hostile, to prevailing practices and policies.[10]

Another distorting influence can arise from pressure groups whose special interests may be furthered by government intervention.[11] As a result, such groups often undertake politically effective efforts to emphasize and exaggerate both the shortcomings of the market and the social benefits to be obtained from government action. Examples are provided by the political pressure of teachers' unions in favor of increased government funds for education, the trucking industry and teamsters' union in favor of various restrictions to limit competition in surface transportation, and the airline industry (at least, the competitively weaker firms) in its prior opposition to deregulation of routes and fares.[12]

A further distorting effect arises from the tendency of government—especially, but not exclusively, the bureaucracy—to be hypersensitive to market shortcomings in the optimistic belief that it (the bureaucracy, or the legislature) possesses the means to remedy them. That the Occupational Safety and Health Administration tends to seek and even exaggerate potential dangers presented by the workplace, or that the Food and Drug Administration (FDA) tends to be more concerned about the dangers of allowing pharmaceutical products on the market too soon rather than too late, reflects these agencies' own inevitable occupational hazards.

In Europe and other parts of the world, to a much greater extent than in the United States, a third influence has tended to exaggerate the market's shortcomings—namely, the intellectual and cultural legacy of socialist ideology in Western European political parties and trade unions, as well as in the Third World. The basic socialist premise that capitalism is inherently prone to instability, exploitation, and inequity provides a strong predisposition to seek and to find confirmatory evidence. The power of a self-confirming hypothesis is not less in this context than in others.

It is noteworthy and significant that this disposition, pervasive and potent in the period from 1950 through the 1970s, dramatically changed in the 1980s. Conservative administrations, oriented toward restraints on government and increased scope for the functioning of markets, produced a sharp reversal in the direction of public policy in the United States, the United Kingdom, and Germany. Even the socialist government of François Mitterand in France adopted policies that encourage and endorse capitalist markets (for example, in removing or reducing wage and price controls, privatizing businesses that had only recently been nationalized, and acknowledging the benefits of competition and free markets). Within the emerging European Community, national barriers to the effective operation of capital, labor, and product markets are being pervasively removed, although the barriers facing external markets seem likely to be maintained if not raised. And in the formerly Communist Second World, market-oriented, systemic reforms are uniformly endorsed, although progress in implementing them has differed widely in China, Eastern Europe, Russia, Ukraine, and the other republics of the former Soviet Union.[13]

Whether these changes in policy direction will be permanent remains to be seen. Even if they endure, the types of distorting influences described earlier sometimes result in presumptions that certain events are typical and frequent, when they are actually rare. In statistical terminology, events that are "outliers" are instead interpreted as though they were "averages"—hence, representatives of the central tendencies of the underlying phenomena. Where this process operates, the result is that perceived estimates of market failure may be systematically different from their true values, because the triggering or newsworthy event, though it is actual, does not represent the central tendency or relative frequency it purports to.

Perceptions and Reality: A Formal Illustration

This view of the process by which perceptions may diverge from reality can be expressed formally by specifying a perceptions function of the following simple form:

$$\hat{Q} = Q_a + Q_t \,,$$

where $\hat{Q}$ is the perceived level of market failure, Q_a is the actual or true level, and Q_t is a transitory disturbance introduced by the several types of distorting influences previously discussed. Consequently, the disturbance term, Q_t, may not have a zero mean, but instead may be systematically biased.[14] Nonmarket demand will be excessive because it responds to the perceived market failure, $\hat{Q}$, rather than the actual one, Q_a. An example of the Q_t distortion is provided by the media's depiction of the imperfect working of the "market" for admissions to American medical schools. The *New York Times*, in a featured story several years ago, reported that there were 340,000 applications for only 16,700 places in first-year medical classes at the nation's 126 medical schools. Based on these statistics, the conclusion was reached that "the chance of getting into medical school is about 1 in 21 nationwide."[15]

The striking and hence newsworthy implication of the story was that the system was grossly imperfect, that the outcome was (presumably) both inequitable and inefficient (because applications and career choices were presumably not based on awareness of such extraordinarily unfavorable odds), and that something ought to be done about it (by implication, through government regulation).

The *Times* article failed to report that, based on data from the preceding year, each medical school applicant filed an average of 9.2 applications! On this basis, the actual chance of admission to medical school would be about 1 in 2.2; 45 percent of the applicants could expect to be admitted. The accurate figures were distinctly unnewsworthy!

It may be conjectured that public "perceptions," $\hat{Q}$, of the system were influenced as much by the Q_t distortion in the *Times* article as by the "true" value, Q_a, of the admissions probabilities.[16]

It is worth noting that, of the several distorting influences described earlier, two may generate countervailing forces that can offset and perhaps reverse the tendency to exaggerate market failures. For example, pressure groups that seek government intervention to remedy market shortcomings may be neutralized or outmatched by opposing groups that prefer the market's unregulated outcomes: industry pressure groups that expect to benefit from regulatory intervention may be opposed by consumer groups that seek to preserve competition (and vice versa).

And the media, if free and uncontrolled, may find newsworthiness in the miscarriages of government no less than of the marketplace: corruption, nepotism, waste, conflicts of interest, and so on. Examples are provided by Watergate, Abscam, Medicaid fraud, Defense Department procurement of $7,500 coffee brewers and $500 wrenches, and the manifold other instances of waste in government procurement. Government failures, as well as market failures, thus provide opportunities for newsworthy exaggerations. Hence, the disturbance term, Q_t, may assume negative, as well as positive, values. To the extent that the newsworthy is simply whatever is unusual, the result may be a tendency to oscillate between overemphasis on market failures and exaggeration of government failures, rather than to describe either of them accurately. However, if the press and the other media are more disposed to seek and expose the vagaries of the market than those of government, the oscillations will not average out to the true value, Q_a, in the long run.[17]

Thus, Q_t may be greater than zero at one time and less at another. Perceptions will be off the mark in both cases, but in different directions. Until at least the late 1970s, the experience in the United States and Western Europe suggests that influences tending to exaggerate perceptions of market failure seem to have been politically more influential than those in opposition. Since 1980, this bias seems to have been redressed.

In sum, if the process that nurtures perceptions of market failures yields distorted estimates, then the demand for nonmarket intervention and activities can be excessive, thereby leading to various nonmarket failures and government deficiencies. Underlying this conclusion, of course, is the assumption that, in democratic systems, the political process generally responds to public perceptions. Consequently, if perceptions are distorted, the response of government will be accordingly deformed.[18]

Against this background of nonmarket demand conditions, the demand for nonmarket activities can be presumed to rise with perceptions of market failures—specifically, with the perceived existence of externalities, valued public goods, monopolistic markets, market imperfections, and distributional inequities.[19]

The Conditions of Nonmarket Supply

As with the conditions of nonmarket demand, nonmarket supply is associated with several characteristics that distinguish it from market supply and contribute to nonmarket failures:

1. Difficulty in defining and measuring output

Nonmarket outputs are often hard to define in principle, ill-defined in practice, and extremely difficult to measure as to quantity or to evaluate as to quality. This, of course, is why nonmarket outputs are measured in the national accounts as the value of the inputs used in producing them. Nonmarket outputs are usually intermediate products that are, at best, only proxies for the intended final output—for example, restrictions or prohibitions on the distribution of drugs and foods by the FDA; licenses issued or rejected by the Federal Communications Commission; forces and equipment developed and employed by the military services; and cases processed and payments disbursed by health and welfare agencies. In each instance, the extent to which the intermediate nonmarket product contributes to the intended final output is elusive and difficult to measure.

The quality of nonmarket output is especially hard to ascertain, in part because information is lacking about output quality—information that would, in the case of marketed outputs, be transmitted to producers by consumer behavior and choice. Consider, for example, the difficulty of determining whether the quality of education, or welfare programs, or environmental regulation, or food and drug regulation, is better or worse now than five or six years ago.

Of course, difficulty of measurement varies widely among nonmarket outputs. For example, the U.S. Postal Service can be readily compared in its performance (with respect to costs and service) with Federal Express; public schools can be compared, although not without difficulty, with private and parochial schools; and police departments can be compared, also with some difficulty, with private security agencies.

More typically, however, appropriate metrics for nonmarket outputs (e.g., defense, regulatory activities, social welfare programs) are elusive and arguable. In general, measuring nonmarket outputs by their inputs is accepted because direct measurement of the output value is so difficult.

2. Single-source production

Nonmarket outputs in government are usually produced by a single agency whose exclusive cognizance (monopoly) in a particular field is legislatively mandated, administratively accepted, or both (for example, the regulatory agencies, the National Aeronautics and Space Agency's role in space, and the public school system, with only very limited competition provided in the latter case by private and parochial schools). It is rare that this exclusivity is contested. Where it is (for example, between the air force and the army in providing some forms of battlefield air support), resolution is frequently on grounds unrelated to output efficiency or quality. Thus, the absence of sustained competition contributes to the difficulty of evaluating the quality of nonmarket output.

3. *Uncertainty of production technology*
The technology of producing nonmarket outputs is frequently unknown, or, if known, is associated with considerable uncertainty and ambiguity. An example of uncertain technology in the educational domain is provided by the Coleman report and other studies that evaluate student performance by reference to standardized test scores. These studies leave very little in the variance of student academic performance to be accounted for by such variables as class size or expenditures per pupil or teacher/pupil ratios, once proper allowance has been made for the social and economic status of student and family. Yet we know very little about how to "produce" education, and indeed what precisely the product consists of. For example, there is disagreement as to whether the cognitive and verbal skills measured by the standardized tests constitute the proper set of educational objectives to be sought. Even if this were agreed upon, our understanding is remarkably limited concerning the mix of curriculum, types and training of teachers, classroom or field experience and application, learning by doing, and the other ingredients of educational technology best suited to providing the educational product.

In the national security domain, where it is commonly assumed that technology is both advanced and well understood, we have at best only a limited understanding of the technical (production-function) relationships between inputs (of military equipment, manpower, training, logistics support, command, control, communications, and intelligence) and the intended final output of national security. More narrowly and more technically, the mix of strategic defensive and offensive capabilities that is best suited to

producing efficient and effective deterrence is poorly understood and widely disputed.

More insubstantial still is our understanding of the technologies associated with producing such other nonmarket
outputs as social welfare through the provision of welfare
services and transfer payments (without thereby creating
perverse effects on labor supply and on the psychological
well-being and motivations of recipients), or providing food
and drug regulations that adequately and properly allow
for the risks facing potential consumers (without thereby
introducing sharply perverse incentives for further research
and development in the pharmaceutical industry).

4. *Absence of bottom-line and termination mechanism*
Nonmarket output is generally not connected with any bottom line for evaluating performance comparable to the
profit and loss statement of market output. Closely related
to this absence of a bottom line is the absence of a reliable
mechanism for terminating nonmarket activities when they
are unsuccessful.

Thus, many of the conditions and characteristics associated with the supply of nonmarket goods and services may
contribute to various shortcomings in their production. This
does not gainsay the fact that the government is predominantly staffed by conscientious individuals and agencies
principally motivated to do a competent job, although the
conditions of nonmarket supply may sometimes cause this
motivation to go awry.

With these characteristics of nonmarket supply as background, it seems reasonable to posit the existence of a functional mechanism for nonmarket activities analogous to the
positively sloped supply curve for market activities. On this
premise, the supply of nonmarket outputs (measured, *faute
de mieux*, by the costs and budgets expended in producing
them) will tend to rise as average government wage rates

(represented, say, by average civil service pay scales) rise and as tax yields rise. When government pay scales rise in relative terms, staffs of government agencies will grow and the total costs they expend (i.e., the standard metric for nonmarket supply) will rise. Also when tax yields rise and public revenues increase, we may assume that aggregate nonmarket supply will rise while absorbing the added revenues. (Conversely, such reforms as California's Proposition 13, and other limits on taxation, will tend to restrict and discourage nonmarket activities.)

Finally, it seems reasonable to assume that the supply of nonmarket activity is positively affected by national income and by government revenues, these being generally correlated with one another. As national income rises, yielding greater public revenues, the supply of (i.e., costs expended on) nonmarket activities will tend to rise in response. New programs will be generated, or existing programs expanded, to absorb the additional resources that have become available. Clearly, some nonmarket activities are more likely to expand than others; for example, perhaps health and educational and environmental programs are more likely to grow with increased national income than are redistributive welfare programs, and the reverse is likely to happen when income falls.[20] Nevertheless, there will probably be a tendency for aggregate nonmarket supply to rise and fall as income rises and falls.

Notes

1. Milton Friedman refers to these collaborating parties as the "iron triangle" of public policy. See Friedman (1984). The same line of argument underlies George Stigler's theory of government regulation (see Stigler, 1971).

2. Feldstein (1980, 6).

3. *Universal Health Care Almanac* (1992).

4. Ibid., p. 4.

5. See Downs (1965).

6. See Feldstein (1980).

7. 1992 data obtained from the Department of Health and Human Services, and the Department of Agriculture. Veterans' data comparable to the 1980 figures were not available for 1992.

8. Feldstein (1980).

9. See Coddington (1975, 151–163), cited in Kantor (1979, 1429).

10. Cf. Rothman and Lichter (1985).

11. See also Stigler, 1971.

12. Describing the point in its French manifestation, Peyrefitte (1976, 319) makes the following comment: "Public administration belongs to civil servants. But additionally, religion belongs to the clergy, health to physicians, education to teachers, intelligence to intellectuals, and chairmanships to Polytechniciens."

13. A compelling testimonial to these dramatic changes is summarized in the following assessment by a commentator who in the past has not usually favored promarket positions, Robert Heilbronner (1989): The Soviet Union [sic], China, and Eastern Europe have given us the clearest possible proof that capitalism organizes the material affairs of humankind more satisfactorily than socialism; that however inequitably or irresponsibly the marketplace may distribute goods, it does so better than the queues of a planned economy.

14. This is not inconsistent with the view that, even if Q_t were equal to zero, society might still be more concerned with (and choose to devote more resources to) the outliers than with the average value. A skewed social-loss function might well be applied to a normal distribution of events or outcomes having a zero mean. However, in this case, society would be proceeding on the basis of accurate, instead of distorted, information: perceptions and reality would be identical. With the previously described mechanism, they would not be.

15. See "Odds against Medical-School Admission Exaggerated," *New England Journal of Medicine*, May 1, 1980.

16. The nuclear reactor accident at Three Mile Island in 1979 provides another example. As a result of the news media's treat-

ment of the accident, the public's perception of the chance of a serious meltdown in the reactor's core was probably as high as 10 percent, or at least 1 percent. In fact, the chance was probably never greater than .001–.0001. If we denote the negative externalities associated with an actual meltdown as X_a, and assume that $X_a=.0001$, then the perceived externalities, x, given these probability assumptions, would be $X_a(10^{-2})$, and the transitory distortion represented by X_t would be 99 times the true value, X_a.

17. As an indication that this premise may, in fact, be warranted, see Rothman and Lichter (1985).

18. See appendix A for further discussion of the demand for nonmarket activities and how demand is influenced by perceptions of market failures.

19. Also, see appendix A for further discussion of the nonmarket demand function and its interaction with nonmarket supply.

20. See appendix A for further discussion of the nonmarket supply function.

4   Nonmarket Failure: Types, Sources, and Mechanisms

The demand and supply characteristics of nonmarket activities described in chapter 3 interact in ways that can be expressed in formal terms as outlined in appendix A. These relationships can, in turn, be used to analyze the actual level of nonmarket activity that will be demanded and supplied and the mechanisms by which the two are, or may be, brought into balance. Appendix A also describes this process. In this chapter, we discuss the plausibility of these relationships and the means by which the expected level of nonmarket activity can be inferred from them.

The expected level of nonmarket activity (or alternative levels, because several equilibria between nonmarket demands and supplies are possible) is likely to embody various shortcomings when judged by the efficiency and distributional criteria applied in chapter 2 to evaluate market outcomes. These sources and types of nonmarket failures are as intimately and inextricably linked to nonmarket activities as the sources and types of failure described in chapter 2 are linked to market activities. The aim of this chapter is to elaborate these nonmarket failures in a manner that facilitates their comparison with the market failures discussed in chapter 2.

Nonmarket Demand and Supply Relationships, and Equilibria between Them

The demand for nonmarket activities can be viewed as resulting from the perceived failures of the market as described in chapters 2 and 3, as well as certain other contextual parameters that will be noted. Thus, aggregate demand for nonmarket activities in general, or the demand for particular types of nonmarket activities (such as environmental regulation by government, health care for the aged, etc.), will be greater to the extent that the public perceives the following market failures to prevail: that the externalities resulting from market activities are substantial; that a high degree of monopoly is associated with the production and sale of market output; that imperfections in the market are rife; and that inequitable distributional benefits result from market activities. These determining or independent variables, it will be recalled, relate to perceptions about the precise sources of market failures, as described in chapter 2.

In addition, certain contextual variables will also influence the demand for nonmarket activity—namely, the level of national income; the prevailing level of taxes; and the costs that are associated with nonmarket activities. For example, as national income and output grow, the demand for nonmarket output can generally be expected to rise, as it does for market outputs. In other words, when people or the economy as a whole receive and produce more, this increase will encourage and permit higher demands for nonmarket, as well as for market, output and activities. At least this will occur for some types of nonmarket output. For example, the demand for public goods and quasi-public goods (scientific and space research, roads and nationwide transportation, even national defense) is likely to increase as the economy can afford more of them. While this will not necessarily apply to all nonmarket demands (for example, the demand for redistributive social programs may decline with higher real income levels, and exogenous changes such as a change in external security threats can have a sharply countervailing effect on the demand for national defense), this relationship is likely to characterize nonmarket demand in the aggregate.[1] In economic terminology, the income elasticity of demand for nonmarket output is positive although its magnitude may be greater or less than unity.

On the other hand, higher tax rates and higher costs associated with nonmarket activities will tend to depress the level of nonmarket demand: If taxes are raised, people will generally be disposed to restrict their demands for nonmarket activity to the extent that they view the tax rate as a sort of a "tax price" associated with nonmarket activity. If taxpayers recognize a link between increases in nonmarket activities and increases in taxes, they will tend to limit their demands for additional nonmarket activities.

In addition, to the extent that the unit costs associated with nonmarket activity rise (which might, for example, be indicated by changes in prevailing salaries in government service), taxpayers (i.e., voters) may be disposed to limit their demands for nonmarket activity. Thus, if government wage rates rise relative to nongovernment wages, public reactions will tend to put a brake on demands for nonmarket activities.

Thus, various factors, relating both to perceptions about market shortcomings and to exogenous, contextual circumstances, will tend to boost nonmarket demand, while other factors will tend to restrain it.

In turn, the supply of nonmarket activities can be thought of as depending on the particular characteristics of nonmarket supply described in chapter 3, as well as on certain other contextual or exogenous variables. If we characterize the supply of nonmarket activities in terms of the costs incurred in producing them, then the supply of nonmarket activities in the aggregate, or of specific types of nonmarket activity (for example, defense or regulatory functions by government), will tend to be higher when the measurement of performance and output of these activities is imprecise. More inputs (costs) will be incurred in producing these outputs when their quality and quantity are less amenable to measurement than when they are more so. The excess can be thought of as waste resulting from the absence of cost discipline that a precise metric would impose.

Nonmarket supply will also tend to be high when nonmarket activities are engaged in by government without the challenge and discipline imposed by competitive activities conducted either within government or in the market sector.[2] In accord with the discussion in chapter 3, we are assuming that the existence of activities that compete with those provided in the nonmarket sector will tend to promote efficiency by the latter.

Finally, where technology that is embodied in the production of nonmarket output is highly uncertain—one of the characteristics of much nonmarket output discussed in chapter 3—the costs of nonmarket supply will also tend to be high. Because of such technological uncertainty, substantial costs may be incurred with limited tangible output. On the other hand, if the uncertainty turns out to be beneficent—that is, if the outputs turn out to be higher than were originally expected from a specified set of inputs—it is plausible that the cognizant nonmarket agency will be disposed to absorb or inflate its ancillary costs. The organizational incentives typically prevailing in nonmarket organizations predispose them to use prior appropriations rather than return them to the Treasury as "miscellaneous receipts." In consequence, the cost implications of technological uncertainty are likely to be skewed toward rising budget costs of conducting nonmarket activities.

It seems also likely that the contextual variables referred to in the discussion of demand—namely, the prevailing level of national income, tax rates, and personnel costs of government activities—will tend to raise the supply costs of nonmarket functions.

Because the factors determining nonmarket demand and supply are numerous and complex, the mechanism by which the two are brought into balance is also likely to be complex.

A general, if often weak, political mechanism operates to correct divergences between aggregate nonmarket demands and supplies, as well as between particular nonmarket demands and supplies. For example, if nonmarket demand exceeds nonmarket supply, there will be a tendency—perhaps only a weak one—for financial and budgetary processes to enact higher government spending and higher tax rates, respectively, thereby enabling nonmarket supply to increase and also tending to reduce demand for nonmarket activity. As the tax-paying public realizes that satisfying its tastes for increased nonmarket output will raise the tax burden, nonmarket demand will be discouraged—again, perhaps only modestly.

Conversely, if nonmarket supply exceeds demand, elected officials and the political process in general will be inclined to mediate the excess supply by lowering relative government pay scales and perhaps by lowering taxes. The resulting tendency is to restrain nonmarket supply and to boost nonmarket demand, thus tending toward a balance between the two.

While this account abstracts and simplifies processes that are typically more complex and less predictable, it suggests the adjustment mechanism that is operative.

Two points should be noted in concluding this discussion of the adjustment mechanism. First, the mechanism by which nonmarket demand and supply are brought into balance is weak and unreliable. It is essentially a political process characterized by lags, bottlenecks, coalitions, log-rolling, and the other fuzzy attributes of political behavior. Consequently, imbalances between nonmarket demand and nonmarket supply may persist for long periods of time. Disequilibrium may be more typical of the relation between them than equilibrium.

Second, even when a balance between nonmarket demand and supply prevails, the balance is likely to be characterized by pervasive inefficiencies and inequities. The reason is that nonmarket demands and supplies themselves, whether in equilibrium or not, already embody inefficiencies or inequities—that is, they already entail nonmarket failures. For reasons described earlier, nonmarket demands may be distorted by the inaccuracies of perceived market failures. Also, nonmarket supply may, and indeed is likely to, entail waste of resources due to technological uncertainty and to various perverse organizational phenomena characterizing nonmarket administering agencies. Nonmarket supply may also involve maldistribution of benefits and costs as an outgrowth of the normal operation of interest-group politics.

Nonmarket failures in governmental performance result no less directly from the characteristics of nonmarket demand and supply than the failures of the market result from the characteristics of market demand and supply. Hence, the choice between markets and governments is fundamentally a choice between imperfect alternatives.

Sources and Types of Nonmarket Failure

Four principal sources and types of nonmarket failure result from the several distinctive characteristics of nonmarket demand and supply. Because these nonmarket failures are embedded in the conditions determining the demand and supply of nonmarket activities, the failures themselves are likely to arise regardless of the point at which equilibrium between demand and supply is established.[3]

The Disjunction between Costs and Revenues: Redundant and Rising Costs

The predominant and ineluctable source of nonmarket failure lies precisely in those circumstances that provide the rationale for nonmarket activity in the first place. Markets link, however imperfectly, the costs of producing or conducting an activity to the income that sustains it. This link is provided by the prices charged for the marketed output and paid by consumers who can choose whether and what to buy. Nonmarket activity removes this link because the revenues that sustain nonmarket activities are derived from nonprice sources—namely, from taxes paid to government, or from donations or other nonpriced revenue sources provided to government or to other nonmarket institutions besides government.

Thus, the absence of this crucial link separates the adequacy and value of nonmarket output from the cost of producing it. The disjunction between them means that the scope for misallocation of resources is enormously increased. Where the revenues that sustain an activity are unrelated to the costs of producing it, more resources may be used than necessary to produce a given output, or more of the nonmarket activity may be provided than is warranted by the original market-failure reason for undertaking it in the first place. Inefficiencies are encouraged because the costs of producing an activity are disconnected from the revenues that sustain it.

Whether policy takes the form of regulation, administering transfer payments, or direct production of public goods, there is a resulting tendency for nonmarket activities to exhibit redundant costs (X-inefficiency)—that is, for production to take place *within* production possibility frontiers—and for costs to rise over time. If technological possibilities exist for lowering cost functions, raising productivity, or realizing economies of scale, these opportunities are more likely to be ignored or less likely to be exploited fully by nonmarket than by market activities. Change is troublesome, the costs of not changing are low, and the possible gains from changing are uncertain. Nonmarket failure, in the form of technically inefficient production and redundant costs, is the result. Moreover, these redundancies may well increase over time.[4]

The sources of these nonmarket failures lie in the demand and supply characteristics associated with nonmarket output. As public awareness of the inadequacies of market outcomes grows, demands for remedial action intensify. Dissatisfaction with existing circumstances may result in misperceiving the cause as a market failure, instead of something more intractable, such as genetics, physical laws, or resistant sociology. With rewards frequently accruing in the political arena to publicizing a problem and then initiating action as an ostensible remedy, nonmarket activities may be authorized that have quite infeasible objectives. Objectives may be internally inconsistent—for example, bringing all students' reading scores up to the mean; or minimizing the time individuals are unemployed while maximizing their earnings; or providing foreign aid to accord with need, but also to provide incentives for sustained development. Or objectives may be specified for which no known technology exists, for example, providing dignified work for people with low IQs, or training people with IQs of 70 to be draftsmen, or achieving a cure for cancer or AIDS by an unrealistically early date.[5] Redundant costs may result at *any* positive level of nonmarket output.[6]

Redundant costs may also result from the difficulty of measuring output, and the resulting need and opportunity to establish agency goals that may be quite remote from the intended ones—namely, the internalities that become accepted as proxies for nonmarket output.[7] The cost-inflating effect of internalities may endure because nonmarket activity is conducted without competition. Or redundant costs may rise over time because of the absence of a reliable termination mechanism for nonmarket output, thereby allowing agency managers to move toward greater indulgence of internal agency goals.

Those responsible for market activities usually have an incentive to expand production and to lower costs over time, because of actual or potential competition or because of opportunities for additional profits. By contrast, those responsible for nonmarket production may be spurred to increase costs (for example, staff), or to increase output even if its incremental value is less than incremental costs (for example, the case of public television in West Germany, which ostensibly sought to maximize gross rather than net revenues), resulting in redundant costs that grow over time.[8] These tendencies toward redundant and rising costs were described by a departing director of the United Nation's Food and Agriculture Organization with reference to his own organization: "Eighty percent of its budget is destined to pay for a gigantic centralized bureaucracy in Rome, 11 percent to put out publications that no one reads, and the remaining 9 percent to holding meetings and for travel expenses that are largely unnecessary."[9]

The details of this example may be extreme, but the general picture probably has wide applicability to nonmarket agencies and activities. Similar charges, and in some instances even more egregious ones, have been directed at the United Nations Educational, Scientific and Cultural Organization (UNESCO) to justify recent decisions by the United

States, the United Kingdom, and other countries to with-
draw from it. The occurrence of substantial cost growth in
public sector projects has been studied and documented in
detail. For example, actual costs of major weapons systems
developed in the 1950s, 1960s, and 1970s rose from their
originally estimated costs by 90 percent, 40 percent, and 30
percent, respectively. Underestimates of actual costs in the
1980s were about the same as those in the 1970s. Construction costs of other public sector projects (for highways,
public buildings, water projects) also exhibited substantial
and comparable growth between initiation and completion.
However, it should also be noted that some private sector
projects in the market domain—for example, major construction projects and energy plants—have experienced
even greater cost growth before completion than did the
public sector projects.[10]

Internalities and Organizational Goals

To conduct their activities, all operating agencies require
certain explicit standards. This requirement does not principally arise from an agency's need to justify its activities
externally, but rather from the practical problems associated
with internal, day-to-day management and operations:
evaluating personnel; determining salaries, promotions, and
perquisites; comparing subunits within the agency to assist
management in allocating budgets, offices, parking spaces;
and so on.[11] Lacking the direct-performance indicators available to market organizations from consumer behavior, market shares, and the profit and loss bottom line, public
agencies must develop their own standards. These standards are what I shall call *internalities*: the goals that apply
within nonmarket organizations to guide, regulate, and
evaluate agency performance and the performance of
agency personnel. I refer to these internalities synony-

mously as private organizational goals because they (rather than, or at least in addition to, the public purposes stipulated in the agency's assigned responsibilities) provide the motivation behind individual and collective behavior within the agency. Thus, public agencies have private internal goals, and these provide or influence the agency's real agenda. This structure of rewards and penalties constitutes what Arrow refers to as "an internal version of the price system."[12]

It is true, of course, that market organizations also must develop their own internal standards in order to regulate the same quotidian functions required for the management of any organization. But there is an important difference. The internal standards of market organizations are related, even if indirectly, to meeting a market test, to responding to or anticipating consumer behavior, to contributing to the firm's bottom line. Sales, revenues, and costs materially affect the internal standards of market organizations. For market organizations, the internal version of the price system must be connected to the external price system. If the two are disconnected, the survival of a market organization will be jeopardized by the response of consumers, competitors, stockholders, and potential raiders, even in imperfect markets.

The situation of nonmarket organizations is different because the supply and demand characteristics associated with their output are different. Because measures of output are often so hard to define, because feedback and signaling from "consumers" are lacking or unreliable, internal standards for nonmarket organizations cannot be derived from these sources. Furthermore, because there are usually no competing producers, the incentive created by competition to develop internal standards that will control costs is weakened. Under these circumstances, nonmarket agencies often develop internalities that do not bear a very clear or reliable connection with the ostensible public purpose that the agencies were intended to serve.

In formal terms, internalities or organizational goals become elements in the utility functions that agency personnel seek to maximize. Hence, internalities affect the results of nonmarket activities as predictably and appreciably as externalities affect the results of market activites. In both instances, divergences result between actual outcomes and socially preferable ones. The existence of externalities means that some *social* costs and benefits are not included in the calculations of *private* decision makers. The existence of internalities means that "private" or *organizational* costs and benefits are likely to dominate the calculations of *public* decision makers. Whereas externalities are central to the theory of market failure, what goes on within public bureaucracies—the internalities that motivate their actions and affect their agenda—is central to the theory of nonmarket failure.

In the market context, externalities result in social demand curves higher or lower than market demand curves, depending on whether the externalities are, respectively, positive or negative. And the levels of market output that result will be, respectively, below or above the socially efficient ones; hence, there is market failure.[13] In the nonmarket context, internalities boost agency supply curves— that is, inflate agency costs—above technically feasible ones, resulting in redundant total costs, higher unit costs, and lower levels of real nonmarket output than the socially efficient ones; hence, there is nonmarket failure.[14]

Whether the nonmarket failure arising from internalities is greater or less than the market failure arising from externalities is an interesting and significant question to which there is no generally satisfactory answer. In principle, the nonmarket sector allows for externalities in determining social demand, and hence comes closer on this count to an efficient level of output.[15] But it does so at a likely cost in terms of the internalities that arise on the supply side. These are reflected in inflated total costs, which push the nonmarket sector away from a socially efficient level, as well as mode, of production. In comparing the effects of internalities and externalities, answering the question of which failure is greater—that of the nonmarket or the market—depends on whether the supply distortions created by internalities in nonmarket output are larger or smaller than the demand distortions created by externalities in market output.

What determines the specific internalities developed by particular nonmarket organizations? Three different hypotheses suggest possible answers.

One hypothesis is that internal standards are based on norms that, when a particular nonmarket organization was originally established, appeared to be reasonable proxies for the elusive final output it was intended to produce.[16] Thereafter, they may become formalized as organizational routines—standard operating procedures that are initially accepted and subsequently retained as a principal measure of the organization's performance. For example, a budget-maximizing internality may arise at the time nonmarket organizations are first established because new organizations have to hire staff and acquire facilities to handle their assigned responsibilities. Through a simple inertial process, the proxy variable (increased staff and budget), which was essential for a particular nonmarket agency at its inception, becomes accepted and retained as a convenient indicator of agency performance.

Although market organizations also establish standard operating procedures, these must generally meet a market test. If the costs of adhering to them exceed those connected with changing them, market pressures will induce alterations. The standard operating procedures of nonmarket organizations must stand up to a different test. Generally, a congressional hearing or scandal of some sort is required for change; and these are likely to be both infrequent and unreliable because they are often not related to agency performance.

A second hypothesis is that particular internalities are selected that maximize the income (and nonincome perquisites) of key agency members. For example, larger budgets as well as administrative concerns that are closely linked to the interests and jurisdictions of particular congressional committees generally mean larger numbers of executive grade jobs in the federal civil service; similarly, the anti-new-technology internality frequently encountered in public schools protects the skills, positions, and incomes of senior faculty members. This hypothesis is close to the view taken in the public choice literature.[17] The third hypothesis is that specific internalities arise because they tend to increase the benefits received by a constituency group that has succeeded in coopting a particular nonmarket organization. Often, the cooptation is by a constituency that the nonmarket agency has been set up to regulate.[18]

Specific Agency Maximands

What are some of the specific internalities that often accompany nonmarket activities and lead to nonmarket failures?

1. Budget growth ("more is better")
Lacking profit as a standard for motivating and evaluating performance, a nonmarket agency may at least tacitly adopt or accept the size of its budget as its principal internality. Performance of the agency's personnel and subunits is then evaluated in terms of their contribution to expanding its budget or protecting it from cuts. Incentives within the agency will develop to reward participants for "justifying

costs rather than reducing them," a characterization that has been applied to the Defense Department and the military services, but surely is not confined to them.[19] It is, for example, standard practice in government agencies—including state as well as federal agencies—to make frantic efforts near the end of each fiscal year to obligate, if not to spend, all remaining funds appropriated for use in the current year. The characteristic agency fear is that existence of unobligated funds, and their mandated return to the Treasury, will translate into a reduction in new appropriations for the ensuing fiscal year. The countermeasures that have been taken by knowledgeable budget officers and examiners to preclude this practice, by disallowing disproportionate year-end obligation of funds, have simply been countered by the anticipatory behavior of agency managers to accelerate the obligation of funds prior to whatever deadline is stipulated. As one observer, commenting on the motivations behind actions of the military services, notes, "The welfare of a service is measured by its budget."[20] Although the comment, without further qualification, is unfair and inaccurate, it surely carries with it an important element of truth.

Thus, the result of a budget internality is likely to be a distortion in the level of agency activity—in other words, a nonmarket failure to produce a socially optimal outcome.[21]

Variants of the budget internality can lead to similar nonmarket failures. For example, managers of Germany's public television and telephone system reportedly asserted in the past that their primary objective was to raise rates and sales so as to maximize *gross* revenues. This, they explained, was necessary to "finance their further growth."[22] If revenue maximization is the internal performance standard, output will rise as long as marginal revenue is positive, again resulting in a socially inappropriate and inefficient outcome—that is, a nonmarket failure.

Another variant of the budget internality is the agency's employment level. A public agency, eschewing or precluded from profit maximization as its objective, may attempt to maximize the size of its staff. For example, British Rail, a nationalized industry and one of the half-dozen largest employers in Britain, has operated under acute pressure from trade unions to maintain high employment levels and avoid so-called redundancies. Operating under such incentives, featherbedding by managers and foremen became a rewarded practice. High employment per unit of service—the converse of high labor productivity—has been sought by the agency, resulting once again in nonmarket failure. Japan's National Railways (JNR) provides a striking contrast. By 1991, four years after JNR was privatized by the Japanese Diet, employment in the railway system had been reduced by 28 percent—from 277,000 in 1987 to 200,000—notwithstanding Japan's tradition of lifetime employment.[23]

2. Technological advance ("new and complex is better")
Often compatible with the budget internality is one relating to advanced, modern, sophisticated, or high technology.[24] Nonmarket agencies, whose activities may be justified in the first instance by one or more of the acknowledged sources of market failure, may establish technical quality as a goal to be sought in agency operations. In medicine, a bias toward Cadillac-quality health care may result, and in the military a sometimes compulsive tendency toward development of the next generation of more sophisticated equipment. Explicit consideration of whether these advances are worth their extra costs is regarded as inappropriate because the operating agencies either are not intended to maximize net revenues (in the case of hospitals) or earn no revenue at all, since they are producing a public good (in the case of military services).[25]

An example is provided by the purchase of disposable syringes by the British national health service in the late 1960s when these gadgets were invented. Their novelty suggested merit. Only later was it demonstrated that repeated use of durable syringes had, in fact, been accompanied by equal or lower rates of attributable infection, and at lower cost.[26]

The development of new systems embodying the latest technology is taken to be an organizational imperative especially, though not exclusively, in the military services. As one practitioner has observed, "In the air force, advancing technology has become a part of the professional ethic."[27] The technological ethic is not confined to the air force. Organizational pressures toward sophistication, complexity, and technological novelty play a powerful role in the acquisition process of other services as well.[28] Nuclear-powered supercarriers are no less an illustration than the B-2 bomber or the advanced fighter aircraft.

The American space program is pervaded by a similar, indeed legislatively encouraged, imperative. From NASA's legislative mandate for "the preservation of the role of the United States as a leader in aeronautical and space science and technology," it has been a short step to formalize the development of novel and complex technology as an internal agency norm, whether or not it seems likely to be efficient.[29]

Although the technological internality is not unique to the military services, it has a special plausibility and justification in this context. The reason is that military agencies, unlike other governmental agencies, must be concerned with the potential advantage that adversaries may acquire if new technology enhances their relative military capabilities. To forestall this eventuality, preoccupation with technological primacy commends itself to military authorities. However understandable, this preoccupation can have perverse consequences, not only in excessive zeal for what is complex and novel, but in mindless opposition to what is simple and familiar. In the Vietnam War, use of a modified propeller-driven cargo aircraft, with long loiter time and a slow stalling speed as a platform for delivering guided munitions as well as airborne artillery, was by far the most efficacious source of American firepower. Yet turning this "gunship" idea into an operating system was delayed five years, largely because of service opposition to what was viewed as a technologically retrograde step!

A bias *against* new technology can, of course, also lead to nonmarket failure. Parts of the American educational system, for example, resist even the experimental use of such new technology as videotaping for presentations to large classes, computer-aided instruction, and performance contracting, all of which might reduce the demand for teachers. Indeed, the education industry's behavior often suggests the opposite of the maxim that "new and complex is better." While a maxim that "familiar and simple is better" may be generally preferable, rigid application of it can have equally perverse effects on performance. Resistance by the education sector to technological advance is similar in quality, although opposite in direction, to the military's frequently uncritical enthusiasm for technology. In both cases, a private organizational goal, an internality, contributes to nonmarket failure.

3. Information acquisition and control ("knowing what others don't know is better")

Another internality that may supplement or supplant the ones previously discussed is the acquisition and control of timely information. Frequently in nonmarket, as well as in market, organizations, information is readily translated into influence and power.[30] In this sense, information is a derived or intermediate internality—an agency norm whose weight depends on its real or presumed connection with enhancing agency influence. Consequently, information becomes valued in its own right—an internality for guiding and evaluating the performance of agency members.

Acquisition and control of information may be particularly important as a goal for agencies involved in foreign policy, because existing constraints already limit the scope for such internalities as budget growth or technological advance. An example is the use of the National Security Council (NSC) framework and the Committee of 40 as means of acquiring exclusive information and, hence, of increasing the influence of the NSC in the 1968–1973 period. The careers of council staff members came to depend on their ability to understand and adjust to the incentives created by this particular internality. Staff members succeeded by demonstrating their ability to collect and protect new information, which White House organizational and procedural rearrangements made possible, for the private use of the NSC, and especially its chief, in his relationships with the president and foreign officials. Acquiring and controlling relevant information for these purposes seemed to become an end in itself, an internal standard motivating behavior in the NSC staff.

The effect of this internality on the conduct of foreign policy, rather than simply on the relative status and influence of the NSC and the State Department, is both obscure and debatable. That this informational internality would lead to nonmarket miscarriages seems likely, since it was connected in no obvious way with the ostensible objective of both agencies—namely, the successful conduct of foreign policy.

The example illustrates a general phenomenon in nonmarket organizations, and especially in government as the largest among them. In the Washington scene, the status and influence of White House staff, cabinet departments, and their secretaries and principal staff often depend on, and are signaled by, their ability to acquire, monitor, and astutely release information pertaining to the current agenda of government. Whether the issue concerns taxes, deficits, arms control, energy, or health, access to and control of information typically rank very high among the implicit standards used internally in evaluating personnel and units of government by their superiors. Both the use and prevention of information leaks are important instruments in the bureaucratic politics of nonmarket agencies.[31] In consequence, effective conduct of an agency's business may be accorded less weight than performing effectively with respect to the informational internality.

Once established, the particular kinds of internalities discussed earlier, as well as other possible ones, become part of the incentive structure to which members of the cognizant nonmarket agency respond. Individual members of the bureaucracy may be, and usually are, conscientious and professional in their desire to do a competent job. But their behavior will be affected by the internalities that govern their agency's behavior, thereby often resulting in nonmarket failure.

In associating these specific types of internalities with nonmarket activity, I do not imply their absence from market activity. For the usual reasons pertaining to more or less imperfectly competitive markets—which, of course, are the only markets that exist—the characteristics of nonmarket activity also apply, to some extent, to market activity. But their extent is likely to be much more limited. Price competition among firms and products as well as competition within firms among managers seeking advancement generally limit the extent of cost-inflating internalities in market activities, as compared with nonmarket activities. Unless the internalities of market organizations contribute to their efficient performance, or at least do not impair it, the organizations will not survive.

What can be said to summarize the difference between the internalities associated with nonmarket output and the externalities associated with market output? Whereas externalities in the market sector are costs and benefits realized by the public but not collectible from or by producers, the internalities associated with nonmarket output are usually *benefits* cherished by producers and paid for by the public as part of the costs of producing the nonmarket output. Consequently, internalities tend to inflate costs and raise supply functions. These shifts, moreover, are likely to increase over time as nonmarket agencies succeed in building special constituencies within the Congress and the public that are the direct beneficiaries, while the costs are spread more broadly over the taxpaying public.

Internalities are thus elements of the private goals of producers: private in the sense that their role is primarily that of satisfying the particular interests of nonmarket producers, rather than contributing to the public sector's intended final output. Such internalities and private goals, often quite remote from an elusive final product, are as frequent and important in nonmarket activities as externalities are in market activities.[32]

Derived Externalities

Government intervention to correct market failure may generate unanticipated side effects, often in areas remote from that in which the public policy was intended to operate. Indeed, there is a high likelihood of such derived externalities, because government tends to operate through large organizations using blunt instruments whose consequences are both far-reaching and difficult to forecast. As the Russian proverb puts it, "When elephants sneeze, other animals get pneumonia."

The unanticipated side effects of nonmarket activities are similar, but not identical, to the externalities of market activities. Externalities in the market domain are side effects (whether anticipated or not) that producers cannot capture when they confer benefits or are obliged to pay when they impose costs.[33] Derived externalities in the nonmarket domain are side effects that are not realized by the agency responsible for creating them, and hence do not affect the agency's calculations or behavior.

The likelihood of externalities is further enhanced by both demand and supply characteristics associated with nonmarket output. Strong political pressure for nonmarket intervention may create an effective demand for action before there is adequate knowledge or time to consider potential side effects. Furthermore, derived externalities are generally more likely to occur later than sooner. Hence, the short time horizon and high time-discounts of political actors predispose them to overlook potential externalities. And, finally, the frequently ill-defined nature of both quantity and quality of nonmarket outputs limits the motivation, as well as the means, for thinking seriously about their potential unintended side effects.

Of course, cost-benefit analysis tries to allow for such externalities, for example, by calculating the expected future benefits of hydroelectric projects so as to include flood control, irrigation, and feeder industries, as well as electric power. But the limitations of such analyses are numerous and well known, resulting in part from the unanticipated nature of some of the side effects.[34]

Derived externalities are hard to anticipate because the consequences of public policies may be far removed from the target. For example, when standards for noise emissions were established by the Environmental Protection Agency to compensate for the market's failure to allow for these externalities, it was unanticipated that one result would be strains (that is, costs) in American foreign policy relations with the French and British over the Concorde supersonic commercial airplane. That an embargo on soybean exports to Japan in 1973 would affect U.S. military-base negotiations in that country was also not anticipated (although perhaps it should have been). That long-standing "Buy America" and other trade restrictions—once again, presumably based on a need for public policy intervention to compensate for market inadequacies—would make it more difficult for debtor countries to service their external debt has been largely ignored, even though it is a relatively straightforward consequence. An example is provided by the U.S. decision in 1984 to apply "voluntary" quotas to exports by Brazil and South Korea of steel and certain other manufactured products to the United States. The aim of this policy was to relieve unemployment in U.S. steel-producing areas in Pennsylvania and Indiana. The externality created by this measure is the impairment of the debt service ability of the two debtor countries, thereby weakening the portfolios of the American banks that hold their debt.

Another instance of derived externalities is provided by public regulation of utilities. Permissible profits are typically calculated on the basis of return on capital, with the intention of holding prices closer to marginal costs, thereby overcoming one source of market failure. But a derived externality often results as an unintended consequence. The regulated utilities may respond by inefficient substitution of capital for labor to raise the allowable profit base.[35] The resulting nonmarket failure may equal or exceed the market failure that regulation was intended to remedy.

Of course, derived externalities may be positive instead of negative. Construction of a North Sea barrier in the Veere inlet, for the safety of the Zeeland population in the Netherlands, meant the loss of mussel and oyster beds but also the start of trout raising, and the end of ocean-going boating but the beginning of a recreational industry based on smaller vessels in the new Veere Lake. None of these outcomes was anticipated when the Veere barrier was originally decided upon.[36]

All of these examples represent a type of nonmarket failure: externalities, whether negative or positive, deriving from a public policy intended to compensate for an existing market failure. They also have in common the characteristic of not having been foreseen at the time the policy was initiated. Clearly, policy choice would be improved if such derived externalities could be taken into account when policy analysis and choice are under way.[37]

Distributional Inequity

As suggested earlier, there is an enormous range of plausible standards for judging equity or fairness. Consider, for example, the wide differences and ambiguities that result from interpreting equity according to each of the following criteria: equity evaluated as equality of opportunity; equity as equality of outcome; equity as perfect equality of outcome *unless* departure from equality is an essential precondition for securing advantages for those who are least favored;[38] equity as a categorical imperative specifying that no personal or individual action is fair unless it can be applied as a general maxim to govern the behavior of others; equity in the sense of horizontal equity (treating equally situated people equally); equity as vertical equity (treating unequally situated people in appropriately unequal ways); equity as Marxian equity ("from each according to ability, to each according to need"); equity according to the Old Testament ("an eye for an eye"); or equity according to the New Testament ("turn the other cheek").

While some of these standards are expressed in terms of penalties (costs), and others in terms of rewards, they do reflect fundamental differences in perspective. Penalties are, of course, negative rewards, and an "eye for an eye" is logically a close cognate of "one good turn deserves another." Among these differing standards, vertical equity has probably received relatively greater attention in the past three decades. This has been reflected in the growth of organizations and legislation seeking protection or preferment for groups that are considered to be particularly vulnerable or disadvantaged because of age, disability, ethnicity, or gender.

Market activities may, and usually do, produce distributional inequities according to several, and perhaps most, of these criteria. While less obvious, it is nonetheless frequently the case that nonmarket activities, whether intended to overcome the distributional inequities of the market or to remedy other inadequacies in the market's performance, may themselves generate distributional inequities. The distributional inequities that result from nonmarket activities are often indexed on power and privilege, rather than on income or wealth.

Public policy measures—whether intended to correct distributional inequities, to regulate industry (because of externalities or increasing returns), to produce public goods, or to redress market imperfections—place authority in the hands of some to be exercised over others. Whether the authority is exercised by the social worker, the welfare-case administrator, the tariff commissioner, the utilities regulator, the securities examiner, or the bank investigator, power is intentionally and inescapably lodged with some and denied to others. The power may be exercised with scruple, compassion, and competence, although it also may not be. It may be subject to checks and balances, depending on the law, on administrative procedures, on the information media, and on other political and social institutions, although these restraints may not be effective.

In any event, such redistribution of power provides opportunities for inequity and abuse. Corrupt practices are one type of abuse—for example, bribery to obtain contracts with foreign governments for sales abroad of weapons or other controlled imports, and import licenses or preferential exchange rates conferred on the relatives, friends, or associates of officials and politicians who exercise discretionary authority. Less conspicuous inequities can result from the decisions of welfare authorities in classifying cases and conferring or withholding aid to fatherless families with dependent children, or to potential recipients of aid for the aged. Anecdotes reflecting the vagaries, perversities, and inequities associated with welfare programs are too numerous to recount, as well as too inexact to yield precise conclusions.

In the specific case of public policies intended to redistribute income, a frictionless, impersonal, and automated redistributive mechanism might avoid the inequitable distribution of power that can result from discretionary authority. But even a sharply progressive tax system which is intended to serve this purpose—reserves considerable room for auditors to exercise judgment and hence power. The same applies to the redistributive expenditure programs mentioned above.

One need not ascribe to those who administer public programs less humane motives than the average to contend that efforts to rectify some inequities may create other ones, or that distributional inequities may result from efforts intended to remedy still other market failures besides distributional ones. For example, land-based missiles, deployed to provide for collective national security, may well expose the collocated population to an inequitably greater risk than that to which the nation as a whole is exposed. It is also true that distributional inequities may be created by graduated taxes (which some of the rich may be more able to avoid than the poor, and which salaried employees are generally less able to avoid than the self-employed), or by some redistributive expenditure programs (such as student loan programs, to which middle income students may have more access than the lower income ones whom the loans are intended to benefit). In general, however, the inequities created by such measures are smaller than the original inequities that such measures relieve.

Nonmarket activities may result in other distributional inequities indexed on income as well as power.[39] It is a truism that any public policy will benefit some and take from others. Indeed, this will ensue whether or not the particular market inadequacy, which gave rise to a nonmarket intervention in the first place, was explicitly distributional in character. Public policy measures will increase the demand for some factors, skills, services, and products and levy costs on others. Those who are specialized in the former will benefit at the expense of those in the latter, by comparison with the previously prevailing situation. If public expenditures are increased for defense or education, justified as instances of vital public goods in the one case or private goods with large and important externalities in the other, organizations and individuals specialized in producing one or the other output will realize increases in their real income.[40]

Consequently, groups that are potentially benefited by a public policy measure intended to compensate for market failure can be expected to urge, and very likely believe, that more compensation is needed to bring about a socially optimal outcome than would otherwise be estimated. Educators, accepting the argument that some government subsidy is necessary to take account of positive externalities ignored by the market, are likely to argue that these externalities are greater than was originally allowed for, and hence warrant a larger subsidy. A similar point applies to the professional and business community concerned with aerospace technology and research and development.[41] The result is likely to be nonmarket failure in the form of a larger public subsidy or a more protective regulatory policy for the benefit of those constituencies that are well organized. Hence, a distributional inequity from the standpoint of non-benefiting groups occurs, even though they may have acknowledged the existence of a market failure and the legitimacy of nonmarket intervention in the first place.[42]

The role of nonmarket activities in producing distributional inequities, whether these are reflected in maldistribution of power or of income, derives from specific demand and supply characteristics associated with nonmarket output.

On the demand side, the principal causal characteristic is heightened public awareness of the inequities generated by the market and the resulting clamor for redistributive programs, often without prior consideration of the inequities that may be generated by these programs themselves.

On the supply side, distributional inequities result from the typical monopoly of nonmarket output in a particular field, and the related absence of a reliable feedback process to monitor agency performance. In the absence of competing producers, those who feel adversely affected, whether as victims of arbitrary administrative authority or as general taxpayers, generally have less direct and less effective means of expressing their dissatisfaction than are available to consumers of marketed output, who can withhold purchases or shift them to other producers. By contrast, those who realize special distributive benefits from particular nonmarket activities are likely to have, or to create, more direct and more effective means for expressing their support, through organized lobbying and advocacy, than are available to consumers in the marketplace.

This does not imply that the inequities of the market are less than those of the nonmarket. However, it does suggest there is an identifiable process by which inequities can result from nonmarket activities, as they also quite clearly result from market activities.

The history of communist systems provides an extreme, but suggestive, illustration. Alleviation, if not eradication, of the inequities of market systems was a fundamental tenet of Marxist-Leninist doctrine and its insistence on the abolition of private property. Yet the extremities in the distribution of power and privilege, as well as of living standards and the quality of life, that actually materialized in these societies represented more flagrant, though less publicized, inequities than those of the market societies they supplanted.[43]

Comparing Market and Nonmarket Failures

The sources and types of nonmarket shortcomings that we have described in this chapter can be tabulated for comparison with the typology of market failure described in chapter 2.

Market failures	Nonmarket failures
1. Externalities and public goods	1. Disjunction between costs and revenues: redundant and rising costs
2. Increasing returns	2. Internalities and organizational goals
3. Market imperfections	3. Derived externalities
4. Distributional inequity (income and wealth)	4. Distributional inequity (power and privilege)

These parallel categories should not be misunderstood. That there are four categories of failures on each side of the ledger does not mean that the collective effects of market and nonmarket failures tend to be equal. Moreover, despite some of the similarities in terminology on the two sides, the nonmarket inadequacies are not the mirror images or "duals" of those associated with market activities. For example, externalities on the market side of the table are qualitatively related to the internalities on the nonmarket side only in the sense that each is a major source of shortcoming in the market and the nonmarket contexts, respectively. Indeed, externalities in the market sector are conceptually much closer to derived externalities than to any other category in the nonmarket side of the ledger.

Figure 4.1 summarizes the discussion in chapters 3 and 4, indicating how particular nonmarket demand and supply conditions contribute to particular types of nonmarket failure. Crosses in figure 4.1 indicate the conditions that have partial effects on the corresponding nonmarket failures; empty cells indicate the absence of such effects.

The tabulation is a convenient device for drawing certain warranted conclusions while avoiding other unwarranted ones.

1. The typical miscarriages of the nonmarket are no less identifiable, characteristic, or predictable than those commonly attributed to the market.

2. The typology of these characteristic nonmarket failures suggests that they are both formidable and relatively neglected.

3. Whether they are more or less formidable than the failures of the market may be ascertainable and demonstrable in some contexts, but is likely to be debatable in others.

4. The choice between markets and governments is not a choice between perfection and imperfection, but between

DEMAND/SUPPLY CONDITIONS / NONMARKET FAILURES	NONMARKET DEMAND CONDITIONS			NONMARKET SUPPLY CONDITIONS			
	INCREASED AWARENESS/ POLITICAL ORGANIZATION	POLITICAL REWARDS/ TIME DISCOUNTS	DECOUPLING	OUTPUT MEASUREMENT	SINGLE SOURCE PRODUCTION	UNCERTAIN TECHNOLOGY	ABSENCE OF TERMINATION MECHANISM
Disjunction between Costs/ Revenues; Redundant and Rising Costs		X	X	X	X	X	X
Internalities and Organizational Goals			X	X	X		X
Derived Externalities	X	X				X	X
Distributional Inequities		X	X		X		X

Figure 4.1
Demand and supply conditions, and nonmarket failures

degrees and types of imperfection, between degrees and types of failure. In many instances, it may be simply a choice between the disagreeable and the intolerable.

Nonprofit Organizations between Markets and Nonmarkets

This book is mainly concerned with elaborating and comparing the characteristics of market and nonmarket organizations, and distinguishing the particular types of shortcomings—that is, failures—to which they are respectively prone, namely, market failure and nonmarket failure. There are, of course, other ways of categorizing enterprises and organizations—for example, public versus private, government versus nongovernment, regulated versus unregulated, and profit versus nonprofit. The categories have some features in common, but are not exactly congruent. For example, enterprises may be publicly owned, yet subject to the discipline of a competitive market and required to realize a profit if they are to grow and if the tenure of present management is to be renewed. Such government-owned, profitmaking companies are rare, but they do exist. Examples include the French firms Aerospatiale and Renault.

On the other hand, enterprises may be privately owned, in a legal and formal sense, yet protected from the market by government regulation or tariffs, and enabled to survive without having to realize a profit because of the subsidies they draw from the government. For example, South Korea's defense industries are privately owned, although government controlled and subsidized. They are, in reality, nonmarket enclaves in an economy that is predominantly market oriented. Moreover, in contrast to most South Korean industries, the privately owned defense industries have been characterized by high costs and low rates of capacity utilization.

Thus, government enterprises may be market organizations, although they usually are not, while private enterprises may be nonmarket ones, although they usually are not. The public versus private distinction is more frequently encountered, especially in Europe, than the market versus nonmarket distinction.[44] Nevertheless, to the extent that the categories are not exactly coterminous, the market/nonmarket distinction seems to me more useful in helping to predict behavior, performance, and the specific types of failures characterizing particular organizations.

Although such crossovers among the categories are infrequent, their occurrence demonstrates that the categories are neither impermeable nor coterminous. In the United States, nonprofit organizations generally lie between market and nonmarket organizations. The question arises whether nonprofit organizations tend to exhibit the characteristics of market or nonmarket organizations, and whether the types and sources of shortfall displayed by nonprofit organizations conform more to those associated with market or nonmarket failure.

Nonprofit organizations (NPOs) represent a small, but not negligible, sector of the American economy, and they cover an enormous diversity of structures, purposes, and operational characteristics. In 1980, total revenues realized by NPOs from contributions, endowments, dues, fees, government transfers, and other private receipts were $160 billion, a sum equal to 6 percent of the GNP.[45] The nonprofit sector employs nearly 10 percent of the American workforce.[46] NPOs include health, education, and research organizations, religious organizations, social service organizations, civic, social, and fraternal organizations, and agencies engaged in the arts, cultural pursuits, and philanthropy.[47] Of total revenues received by NPOs, those engaged in providing health services are by far the largest recipients, accounting for $74 billion of the total in 1980, followed by education and research organizations, which accounted for $37 billion, and religious organizations, whose receipts totaled $18 billion.[48]

Determining exactly where to place nonprofit organizations in the market versus nonmarket categories, or in the spectrum between them, is difficult and ambiguous. Some NPOs operate in a competitive, quasi-market environment. For example, think tanks often compete with one another: RAND sometimes competes with the Institute for Defense Analyses, Battelle Memorial Institute, the Stanford Research Institute, the Brookings Institution, various university-based research and analysis institutes, and occasionally profit-making organizations such as Science Applications, Inc. Nonprofit organizations providing health care also operate in a quasi-market environment that is becoming somewhat more disciplined and competitive than it has been in the past.

Other NPOs—especially foundations, public schools, religious organizations, state universities, and so forth—operate in environments that are quite remote from competitive markets, and hence they fit more naturally in the nonmarket than the market category. The nonmarket is a better description of these NPOs because the special environments in which they operate do not display the classical characteristics of markets, and instead are often either supported by or subject to influence by the governmental nonmarket. In general, most NPOs are therefore subject to the sources and types of nonmarket failure—namely, internalities, redundant and rising costs, derived externalities, and extramarket forms of inequity—rather than to the types and sources of failure associated with market organizations.

A RAND study that dealt with one particular type of nonprofit organization—namely, grant-making foundations including several of the largest private foundations as well as the National Science Foundation—provides some support for the proposition that NPOs seem to fit more comfortably into the category of nonmarket organizations than of market organizations and are subject to nonmarket, rather than market, failures.[49] Through questionnaires and interviews with executives in these foundations, this study arrived at several conclusions concerning the particular nonmarket processes and characteristics that are found in these NPOs.

1. Their decision making is usually not based on explicit, measurable criteria because the purposes they seek to advance are so broad (for example, furthering the progress of science; contributing to improved national health, prosperity, and welfare; furthering the growth of scientific and technical knowledge).

2. The standards they employ for evaluating actions they take both with respect to the outside world (namely, project selection and funding) as well as internally (with respect to the hiring and promotion of staff personnel) are dominated by concern with process rather than product, because these organizations lack a bottom line for calculating how well they are performing.

3. Internal norms, or criteria relating to established and accepted operating procedures in these NPOs, are developed to evaluate personnel; for example, promotions tend to be based on political skills, a network of connections, the ability to avoid doing too much alone, and the ability to deal with large and unclear situations.[50]

4. Lacking the informational feedback that market organizations receive from consumer behavior and sales, nonmarket enterprises in the grant-making field look for guidance concerning projects and priorities to the outside marketplace of ideas and prevailing social concerns; moreover, subjective judgments within the foundations are especially

influential in interpreting the soft information gleaned from these sources.[51]

In sum, by and large and with some notable exceptions, nonprofit organizations tend to conform more closely to the characteristics of the nonmarket than to those of the market and hence are more prone to the types of shortcomings or failures associated with the nonmarket.

Linkage between Market and Nonmarket Failures

Chapters 3 and 4 have presented a framework for analyzing nonmarket failures separately from market failures to facilitate comparison between them, according to criteria of equity as well as efficiency. Yet market and nonmarket failures may sometimes be linked.

Mancur Olson, in his broadbrush treatment *The Rise and Decline of Nations*, argues that markets malfunction most flagrantly when cartels and lobbies are fortified by long tenure and experience.[52] As a result, they can pressure government to undertake action—subsidies, tariffs, tax preferences, quotas, direct expenditures, or tax expenditure programs—that will benefit their collective membership at the expense of the rest of society. In the process, government as well as markets are likely to malfunction, producing outcomes that are both inefficient and inequitable.

Notes

1. The income elasticity of demand for redistribution is subject to conflicting influences. On the one hand, the disposition of the hypothetical "median voter" in favor of redistribution is likely to decline when fewer people are below the poverty line. On the other hand, if the marginal utility of the median voter's own consumption declines as income increases, the relative disposition in favor of redistribution may be enhanced. My guess is that the first tendency is likely to be stronger than the second.

2. Paradoxically, but plausibly, monopoly in nonmarket production will tend to inflate output (i.e., costs) to a budget-maximizing or influence-maximizing level, while monopoly in market production will tend to restrict output to a profit-maximizing level.

3. Cf. appendix A for further discussion of equilibria between nonmarket demand and supply.

4. The term *redundancies* has a different meaning here from that referred to earlier. Clearly, maintaining low productivity to avoid *employment* redundancies, as in the case of British Rail cited earlier, is one source of *cost* redundancies.

5. In the words of one observer, whose comment is all the more insightful because it preceded his own not inconsiderable role as Secretary of the Energy Department, in providing evidence in its support, "[N]ew agencies, from which better things might be hoped, are put under unremitting pressure to produce glamorous new programs—before the necessary analysis has been performed" (Schlesinger, 1968).

6. In effect, demand and supply functions may not intersect, yet the demand for nonmarket activity may still be politically "effective." In the diagram, nonmarket output of, say, q^* will be politically supportable if those receiving the benefits, $\int_0^{q^*} D(q)dq$ are

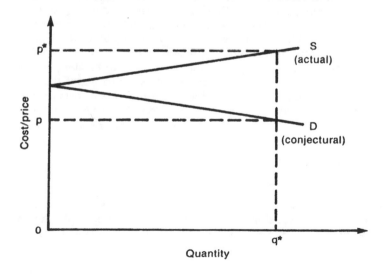

politically more effective (even though they pay nothing or at least pay less than the benefits) than those who pay the full costs, $\int_0^{q*} S(Q)dq$ or at least pay the difference between the full costs and the amount paid by the first group. $q*$ would presumably be established at the point where the marginal effectiveness of political support equals that of political resistance. To avoid tautology requires that the ingredients of political effectiveness (for example, organizational skill, media pressure) for the gainers and the losers can be evaluated independently of the resulting nonmarket activity.

7. See the following discussion and definition of internalities.

8. Hence, cost functions for nonmarket activity are likely to drift upward because of private goals (internalities). This upward drift is what I mean by rising costs. By redundant costs, I mean the tendency of nonmarket activities to be carried on inside, rather than on, the production possibility frontier at any given time. The two tendencies thus relate to dynamic inefficiency and X-inefficiency, respectively.

It is possible to test the hypothesis advanced here that (a) rising costs and (b) redundant costs tend to be associated with nonmarket activities compared with market activities. One might use for this purpose cost data in sectors where production has been carried on in both a market and a nonmarket mode (for example, education, fire protection, housing) within a given country, or in comparisons between market and nonmarket modes in different countries (for example, health care in the United Kingdom and in the United States). Empirical studies of production by market and nonmarket organizations (for example, private versus governmental production in fire protection and in refuse collection) suggest that the former tend to be more efficient and that redundant costs tend to be associated with nonmarket organizations. See Ahlbrandt (1973) and Spann (1977). The results of these and other relevant studies are discussed in chapter 7.

9. International Herald Tribune, April 26, 1976.

10. See Rich and Dews (1986) and Merrow et al. (1979).

11. Much of the organizational behavior literature of the past two decades advances similar points of view. See, for example, March and Simon (1958), Simon (1960), Cyert and March (1963), Downs

(1965), and Allison (1971). See also Schultze (1977), Peacock (1980), and Niskanen (1983).

12. Arrow (1974).

13. Recalling the optimum condition noted earlier (see chapter 2, note 9), if the Σv^s_{mj} are positive, the j units produced under market conditions will be less than is socially optimal; if the Σv^s_{mj} are negative, the j units produced will exceed the social optimum.

14. If the optimum condition were complied with, producing j units of output would be less than is socially optimal in the absence of internalities, because mc^s_j is inflated by the internalities of the nonmarket producers. If cost increments induced by the prevalence of internalities were removed, mc_j would be lower and the optimal level of real nonmarket output would be higher, assuming the valuations placed on the jth unit are correct (see chapter 2, note 9).

15. The Σv^s_{mj} are, in principle, included in determining output decisions in the nonmarket sector.

16. McFadden's attempt to infer what a government agency (namely, the California State Highway Division) is trying to maximize by observing its prior behavior (for example, with respect to project and route selection compared to optimal choices) is in the spirit of this hypothesis. See McFadden (1975).

17. See Niskanen (1971, chap. 1) and Stockfisch (1976). In the general form stated in the text, the second hypothesis begs the questions of which agency members are key and the time horizon over which income maximization is construed. It also begs the more subtle connection between income received while a member is in the agency and the income he or she may look forward to in the private sector. In some cases, the first and second hypotheses lead to similar predictions; for example, both hypotheses are consistent with establishment of budget maximizing as an agency internality. In others, the predictions probably differ; for example, the information-acquisition internality (see following) is hard to reconcile with the first hypothesis.

18. This hypothesis is advanced in Stigler (1971) and applied empirically to transportation and professional licensing. This hypothesis is also suggested by the comment later in this chapter of regulatory agencies and of the constituencies they affect most directly.

19. Defense Science Board quoted in Nimitz (1975).

20. Ibid.

21. Using plausible demand and cost functions, Niskanen (1983) has shown how the budget internality will lead to an output level above the socially efficient one.

22. I am indebted to James Rosse for this example.

23. See Administrative Inspection Bureau (1990).

24. This is not the place to attempt to define precisely what is meant by *high technology*, a subject richly clothed in confusion in both popular and professional discussion. To consider whether the term does, or should, refer to products or processes, novelty or efficiency, costs and/or effectiveness would take us too far afield. For present purposes, I shall conveniently assume that high technology, like a camel, is easy to recognize if difficult to describe.

25. Newhouse (1970) has shown formally how the addition of a quality argument in the maximands of nonprofit hospitals tends toward misallocation of resources in the health care industry. A nonmarket failure results because managers trade off quality against quantity, producing a different product from that which consumers would choose if they were spending the resources that nonprofit hospitals receive from public or philanthropic sources. In the Newhouse model, misallocation is reduced because a nonprofit hospital's choice of high quality is assumed to shift consumer demand upward, thereby adding to the market value of outputs. However, this may not occur. As long as the nonprofit hospital draws a subsidy (from government or philanthropy) based on the presumed market failure (for example, externality) that the subsidy is intended to correct, the hospital can price its output below cost, while indulging its practitioners' taste for quality. The original source of market failure is not thereby redressed.

26. Feldstein (1968).

27. Head and Rokke (1973). The particular attraction in the U.S. Air Force of technological advance as an organizational internality is well known. The process of its adoption is probably an example of the hypothesis concerning initially valid proxies whose validity may have diminished after the proxy had already become accepted and engraved in agency operating routines. For example, when

the Air Force was established as a separate service in 1947, two circumstances impelled it toward emphasizing technological advance as an organizational internality: (a) the two decades of struggle with the U.S. Army to win acceptance of the new aviation technology, independent of artillery and infantry; and (b) the major technological advances achieved during World War II (for example, in radar and nuclear weapons) and the resulting belief that the outcome of a future war "would be determined solely by the technological power of weapons that adversaries could bring to bear in its first moments" (Sapolsky, 1972).

28. Alexander (1976).

29. National Aeronautics and Space Act of 1958, Public Law 85568, Sec. 102 (c)(5).

30. For a more general treatment of the importance of informational access and control in postindustrial society, see Bell (1973).

31. Of course, this internality is not confined to nonmarket organizations, although it may be particularly important in them. For example, in the internal struggle for top executive leadership in the merged Time-Warner Corporation, the victor's triumph was in part attributed to his understanding that to "control the information, [is to] control the power" (Bruck, 1992).

32. The existence of internalities in organizations producing nonmarket outputs can, through the effect of internalities on the costs of producing the nonmarket outputs, be related to the condition for determining an optimal (efficient) level of output. Recalling the notation used in chapter 2, the condition is

$$mc_j^s + \sum_{p=1}^{q} mc_{pj}^s = \sum_{m=1}^{k} v_{mj}^s,$$

where mc_{pj}^s is the marginal cost of the pth internality associated with production of the jth unit of the sth public good. Just as the market lacks a direct mechanism for reaching an optimum in the face of externalities, so the nonmarket lacks any mechanism for reaching an optimum in the face of the internalities shown in the above specification.

This specification is closely related to Stigler's "positive" theory of regulation: a benefit of some outside constituency becomes an agency goal and an argument in the agency maximand. I think

Stigler errs, however, in denying what seems to me a generally valid proposition about public policy intervention: even though cooptation of a regulatory agency frequently occurs *after* the agency gets under way, nonmarket activity is rarely undertaken without a case being first made on normative grounds, based on market failure or distributional equity (Stigler, 1971); see also Posner (1974).

33. See the discussion of market failure in chapter 2.

34. A detailed attempt to internalize such externalities, as well as a candid acknowledgment of the limitations of cost-benefit analysis that tries to do so, is contained in Hirshleifer, DeHaven, and Milliman (1960). Hirschman, in his notion of the "hiding hand," emphasizes the benefits, rather than the costs, of unanticipated consequences from *selected* development projects undertaken by governments. Of course, whether the hand principally hides benefits or costs depends on which development projects are selected for retrospective examination (Hirschman, 1967).

35. Averch and Johnson (1962).

36. See Goeller et al. (1977).

37. To the extent that better analysis can anticipate and calibrate the derived externalities associated with nonmarket output, they become analytically identical to the externalities associated with market output. Hence, the optimum condition for nonmarket output with derived externalities is the same as that specified earlier for market output with externalities. However, determining the $\sum v_{mj}^s$ ex ante may be even harder for nonmarket derived externalities because of the bluntness of nonmarket instruments and the frequent remoteness of their effects both in time and in place.

38. See Rawls (1971, 1303): "All social primary goods—liberty and opportunity, income and wealth, and the bases of self-respect—are to be distributed equally unless an unequal distribution . . . is to the advantage of the least favored."

39. For example, Valerie Bunce includes the distribution of both income and power in evaluating "social inequality" in communist countries. See Bunce (1983).

40. Imposition of nondistorting lump-sum taxation to capture these economic rents is arguable in theory and difficult to realize in practice.

41. A former executive of the General Electric Company has suggested the following matching between certain government organizations and the policy areas, on the one hand, and their business and professional constituencies, on the other:

Government organizations	Related business organizations
Department of Defense, NASA	Defense-space contractors
Department of Agriculture	Farmers; dairy, meat processors
Environmental Protection Agency	Auto manufacturers; electric utilities
Securities and Exchange Commission	Brokers; underwriters; issuers
Interstate Commerce Commission	Railroads; truckers
Federal Communications Commission	Radio and TV stations and networks; cable and pay TV
Tariff Commission	Trade unions; businesses subject to import competition
Food and Drug Administration	Pharmaceutical industry; food and beverage industry
Federal Power Commission	Electric utilities; natural gas producers
Nuclear Regulatory Commission	Atomic energy equipment builders

Note: See Birdzell (1975).

42. The distributional type of nonmarket failure is the core of Stigler's theory of economic regulation. Stigler finds empirical evidence to support this hypothesis in interstate variations in trucking regulation and in occupational licensing. See Stigler (1971).

43. For striking illustrations of the quality of life among the Soviet ruling class and its extraordinary contrast to that of the average Soviet citizen, see Voslensky (1984) and Vishnevskaya (1984). Concerning inequities in Eastern Europe as well as the Soviet Union, see Bunce (1983).

44. As an example, the French journal *Revue Politiques & Management Public* held a symposium entitled "Public, Privé: Espaces et Gestions" ("Public, Private: Turfs and Management") in Lyons in December 1986. The symposium mainly dealt with the differences and similarities between market and nonmarket organizations, although most of the terminology that was used referred to public and private organizations.

45. Most, but not all, receipts of nonprofit organizations represent income transfers, rather than income earned. Hence, this part of their receipts does not constitute value-added and is therefore not a part of the gross national product (Hodgkinson and Weitzman, 1984, 45).

46. Ben-Ner and van Hoomissen (1991).

47. Hodgkinson and Weitzman, op. cit. Since 1979, Professor John Simon of the Yale Law School has directed a detailed study of the scope and effectiveness of NPOs.

48. Ibid.

49. See Eby (1982) and Wolf (1982).

50. See Eby, op. cit., 31–32.

51. Wolf (1982, 10). For more detailed treatment of the nonprofit sector, see Ben-Ner and van Hoomissen (1990).

52. See Olson (1982).

5

Nonmarket Failure and the Analysis of Public Policy

The theory of nonmarket failure presented in chapters 3 and 4 has an important bearing on the emergence and development of the new academic and professional field of public policy analysis. This chapter—a change of pace and focus from the preceding ones—explores the relationship between the theory of nonmarket failure and the practice of public policy analysis. A summary of the origin and development of policy analysis provides background for this discussion.

Since 1970, three or four dozen graduate professional degree programs have been established in the United States to provide training in the emergent field of policy analysis and public management. Among the major institutions offering graduate programs in this field are the University of California at Berkeley, Harvard, Yale, Carnegie Mellon, Columbia, Duke, Michigan, Pennsylvania, Minnesota, Princeton, Rochester, Texas, and the RAND Graduate School of Policy Studies.

These programs award master's or doctoral degrees to about 1,500 graduate students a year.[1] More than 10,000 positions in federal, state, and local government currently carry the professional civil service designation of policy analyst. The private sector, too—especially in large multinational or conglomerate firms that frequently interact with the public sector—has shown an increasing interest in employing public policy graduates. Their skills are viewed as providing either a competitive challenge or a complement to the skills and professional training received by graduates of university schools of business.[2]

Furthermore, the field of policy analysis has achieved the characteristic cachet symbolized by establishment of a professional association—the Association for Public Policy Analysis and Management (APPAM)—in 1979, and an official association journal, *The Journal of Policy Analysis and Management*, established in 1980.

Policy analysis can be defined as the application of scientific methods to problems of policy choice and implementation in domestic, international, and national security affairs. More precisely, the field evolved from the application of the methods of microeconomics to the analysis of defense problems in the 1950s and early 1960s. This application was subsequently extended through the development of planning, programming, and budgeting systems (PPBS), focused on policy issues in such domestic fields as health, energy, and education in the early and late 1960s.[3]

How does this digression on policy analysis relate to the subject of this book, markets and governments? The answer is that the theory of nonmarket failure, which has been elaborated in the preceding chapters, can provide a useful supplement to the standard methods associated with policy analysis.

Policy analysis, as it is usually practiced, proceeds through the following steps:

1. Collecting and analyzing data bearing on the domain under scrutiny (e.g., health care, education, arms trade and arms control, economic development). Usually, this step involves extensive use of quantitative data as well as intensive familiarization with the institutional context of the area. Exposure to the soft, institutional aspects of the area is no less important than exposure to those that are susceptible

to quantitative analysis if the subsequent analysis is to avoid spurious rigor and instead to achieve practicable relevance to public policy.

2. Using this data analysis and institutional understanding, together with relevant theory, to understand the relationships among the variables constituting the domain or the system under study.

3. Building a model that specifies, on the basis of the prior steps, the key relationships between dependent and independent variables. Not only does effective model building depend on immersion in the data and development of a reliable feel for the domain under study but it requires, as well, a sensitivity to the objectives of concern to public policy in the area under investigation. For example, the objectives may be to contain health care costs while avoiding, or at least limiting, adverse effects on quality of care; or to control or counter proliferation of weapons and weapons technology without thereby increasing crisis instability; or to provide incentives for the development of effective new pharmaceuticals without encouraging premature marketing of inadequately tested products. These objectives should be represented as dependent variables or constraints in the analytic model.

4. Formulating, and sometimes inventing, alternative programs or policies intended to further the objectives that the policymaker is responsible for achieving. It is usually essential that the alternative programs or policies include the existing program or policy as the base case, as well as additional options planned or suggested by others, and options devised by the analyst.

5. Finally, evaluating the alternative policies by testing them in the model and comparing their results through performance criteria reflecting the specified objectives described earlier. In general terms, the preferred option or

policy is that which maximizes these objectives for stipulated costs while complying with specified restraints or, alternatively, minimizes the costs of meeting a stipulated level for the objectives while similarly complying with the specified constraints.

What this standard sequence omits is an explicit concern for the vagaries and predictable shortfalls in governmental performance that inevitably arise when fallible agencies, prone to the characteristic structure and behavior of nonmarket organizations, are given responsibility for translating a chosen policy into an operating reality. What is lacking in the standard analytic sequence has been referred to as the "missing chapter" in most policy analyses—namely, a chapter dealing with implementation.[4] It is precisely at this point that the theory of nonmarket failure becomes relevant to the refinement and extension of policy analysis.

Even the most sophisticated policy analyses usually neglect implementation issues. Policy studies rarely raise and almost never answer such questions as *who* would have to do *what* and *when*—with what foreseeable resistance, modifications, and compromises—depending on whether alternative A were chosen rather than B or C. As far as implementation is concerned, the Napoleonic dictum is tacitly accepted: *"On s'engage et puis on voit"* ("Commit, and then wait and see"). Thus, analysts implicitly assume that the costs and benefits, as they have been modeled in the analysis, will not be altered in the process of implementation.

In fact, what typically happens diverges drastically from this assumption. Programs and policies often change radically in the course of implementation. For example, many studies of the development and procurement of new weapons systems illustrate the drastic effects of subsequent implementation difficulties in altering the results that were originally envisaged. To cite one instance, ex post analyses of dozens of weapons systems developed in the United States have shown that, on average, system costs (after allowing for differences in technology, performance, procurement scale, and so on) increased by a factor of three between the time development was begun and delivery was completed.[5]

Our previous discussion of nonmarket failure provides a means of addressing the question of how studies of public policies can better anticipate and remedy implementation difficulties. Systematic consideration of these implementation problems has been properly referred to as the "missing chapter" in standard policy studies because of the typical avoidance of these problems in such studies. The phenomena of nonmarket failure envisage most of the implementation difficulties and shortfalls that this elusive chapter should address.

Interest in implementation issues has increased substantially as the field of policy analysis has matured, and this interest is amply reflected in several recent books and case studies, as well as in the curricula of the graduate schools referred to earlier.[6] This discussion has emphasized the typically large gaps between programs as they were designed and as they eventually were executed, the lack of appropriate methods for anticipating these gaps and taking them into account, and consequently the failure of virtually all policy analyses to address implementation issues systematically.

To move from these justifiable criticisms to improved implementation analysis requires an acceptable paradigm. The preceding treatment of nonmarket failures in chapters 3 and 4 can provide this paradigm—namely, a way of analyzing how public policy (that is, nonmarket) efforts to compensate for market failures may themselves fail to achieve the sought-after ends and fail in predictable ways. Anticipating such nonmarket failures can be invaluable for efforts to avoid them, or for developing mixed market and nonmarket alternatives that will diminish the more undesirable consequences of each.

Policy analysis can deal more effectively with implementation issues by supplementing the standard policy analytic procedures mentioned above with a link to the theory of nonmarket failure discussed in the preceding chapters. The reasons for implementation shortfalls—for costs to rise and effectiveness to fall from the levels they were anticipated to reach—in public policies intended to correct inadequacies of the market lie in the predictable inadequacies of nonmarket activities themselves. Hence, implementation analysis, as a supplement to the procedures usually followed in policy studies, can benefit by applying the theory of nonmarket failure expounded in this book.

The aim of this application is to improve the comparisons that can be made of the costs and effectiveness of alternative public policies and programs, and between them and market solutions, or combinations of market and nonmarket ones. The theory and typology of nonmarket failure can provide a guide to anticipating ways in which the costs of nonmarket programs may rise, or effectiveness decline, for reasons usually overlooked in most policy studies. As a consequence, more useful cost-effectiveness comparisons can be made between market and nonmarket solutions.

Toward this end, it is useful to distinguish two aspects of implementation analysis: (1) descriptive and (2) normative-inventive.

1. The descriptive part of implementation analysis can employ the typology of nonmarket failures outlined earlier as a checklist for comparing the potential miscarriages of various policy alternatives. For example, the following implementation questions can be addressed as a standard part of the analysis of policy alternatives prior to choosing among them:

a. If policy A or B or C were adopted, which government departments, agencies, or bureaus would have to be assigned what precise responsibilities?

b. To the extent these designated agencies are already in existence, instead of new agencies to be created, what are the *internalities and private goals* that now motivate them, and how is agency behavior affected as a result? (If one looks at how these agencies really operate, the following questions arise: How is output actually measured, and how are success and effectiveness in producing it assessed? Are staff members rewarded for adding to or justifying costs, or for reducing them; for generating new technology, or opposing it, or objectively evaluating technology options; for connecting the agency with new information sources while restricting access by nonagency personnel, or for facilitating informational flows to and from other agencies?) If the policies under consideration call for creating new administering agencies, can the corresponding internalities, and the way in which they will influence agency behavior, be anticipated (by the evident connection between particular policies and the interest groups advocating them: for example, between the Strategic Defense Initiative office and the aerospace industry)?

Can agency internalities be modified by program redesign—for example, by risk-sharing or fixed-cost contracts that promote efficiency by government contractors, as well as by administering agencies? How would such procedures affect agency behavior, and over what period?

c. What *externalities* may result from the alternative policies—over what time period and with what likelihoods, perhaps in policy areas remote from the target area of the programs under consideration? For example, in efforts to impose "voluntary" quotas on South Korean and Brazilian steel exports, and Japanese car exports, into the United States, the evident purpose of the policy has been to provide breathing space for the beleaguered domestic U.S. steel and automobile industries, respectively. On the other hand, no systematic consideration was given to the effect that such restrictions would have on South Korea's and Brazil's ability to service the enormous debts they owed to American commercial banks—over $90 billion owed by Brazil, and over $40 billion by South Korea in the mid-1980s; nor in Japan's case was it anticipated that the voluntary quotas would induce Japanese producers to shift toward higher quality, higher technology, and higher priced car exports to the United States. These unintended side effects were foreseeable, but unforeseen and unacknowledged, consequences of the original quotas. From the analyst's point of view, allowing for such unforeseen externalities is an exercise in anticipating what would otherwise be ignored. It exemplifies a derived externality, in terms of the types of nonmarket failure described in chapter 3, but one that can be taken into account in policy analyses, rather than overlooked.

d. Based on the track records of the agencies involved, on scrutiny of alternative policies for the possible existence of inconsistent or otherwise infeasible program objectives, and on considerations covered in (b), can estimates be made of the prospective occurrence of *redundant and rising costs* associated with the assignment of agency responsibilities? Can cost-estimating relationships be calculated (as in the system acquisition example referred to earlier) to express the upward drift in cost functions likely to be encountered over time? In the case of weapons systems development and procurement, such reestimates of the likely increases of costs can provide a more realistic basis for deciding when and whether to proceed with particular systems.

e. Finally, in accord with the way in which each of the policies or programs under consideration would be expected to operate, how much discretionary authority is given, and to whom? As among the alternatives, what changes would ensue in *distribution*, not only in income distribution, but also in the distribution of power that may be exercised by some parts of the public sector over other parts, as well as over the private sector and individual members of the public? (One of the implicit premises of what was labeled "new federalism" is that it was likely to diminish the excessive concentration of power in the federal government, by some devolution of responsibility to state and local levels of government or to the private sector.)

Clearly, many and perhaps most of the foregoing questions are not answerable in precise terms. Answers are instead likely to be judgments and opinions, subject to disagreement by reasonable people even after empirical work to obtain objective information has been done. Nevertheless, even soft answers, which display such divergent judgments, would be valuable adjuncts to the normative dimensions of implementation analysis.

2. The normative-inventive dimension of implementation analysis has three purposes associated with it. One purpose is simply to facilitate evaluation of the specified alternatives with respect to the ease or difficulty of implementing them—of translating "what is good to be done" into an estimate of what actually would get done.[7] In effect, this would amount to an ex post adjustment in the costs and benefits as modeled, before implementation considerations are brought into the analysis.

A second purpose is to facilitate comparison between the actual inadequacies associated with the market and the potential inadequacies associated with implementing the nonmarket remedies under consideration. Juxtaposing the market failures to be remedied and the nonmarket failures to be anticipated from the remedies themselves would permit an assessment that has seldom been attempted in previous policy studies and should be made difficult to avoid in future ones. This comparison is similar to what has been referred to as zero-based budgeting in discussions of planning, programming, and budgeting systems. The inadequacies of a particular market outcome, with little or no public intervention (a zero budget), may be preferable to the inadequacies of the nonmarket remedy.

The third purpose of applying the paradigm of nonmarket failure is to stimulate invention: new ideas for policies and programs, or combinations among those under consideration, or of parts of them, or of entirely different approaches to the problem. A systematic comparison between market failures and nonmarket failures in a particular problem area (the second purpose), and among the potential nonmarket failures associated with various alternative policies (the first purpose), should contribute to a result Dr. Samuel Johnson associated with the prospect of being hanged—that it concentrates the mind wonderfully. Invention of new options, or discovery of ways to improve existing options, can be thereby stimulated. If nonmarket solutions have been needed as countermeasures against market failures, we now need to develop countermeasures against nonmarket failures (hence, "counter-countermeasures" against market failures).

Besides evaluation of the existing set of options, the normative-inventive part of implementation analysis should focus on the following set of questions, which are as important, and as formidable, as the previous set:

a. Are there relatively simple and easily administered fixes in the operation of markets that would sufficiently alleviate the acknowledged market failure to provide an acceptable solution?[8]

b. Can policies be invented that, while recognizing the need for nonmarket interventions because the market's inadequacies are so great (for example, in the case of public goods or of private goods with major externalities), nevertheless try to retain certain valuable characteristics of market solutions (for example, competition by several producers, tangible and public performance measures, beneficiary charges for certain public services, and the equivalent of a profit center mode of operation for operating agencies)? In particular, can mechanisms be devised for the "reprivatization" of certain public services, for example, using publicly funded vouchers for the "purchase" of education, or open bidding on private contracts for waste disposal or postal services?[9]

c. Can improved measures for nonmarket output be devised, so that those nonmarket failures resulting from the lack of a suitable metric can be reduced? For example, can teaching quality be more accurately measured by student improvements registered in standard test scores, rather than by graduate courses on pedagogy completed by teachers? Can tests be made of the connections, or lack thereof, between the intermediate outputs that are often reflected in agency internalities and the final outputs that are publicly mandated and ostensibly sought?

d. Can the internalities (standards, goals) that provide the incentives for individual and agency behavior be revised so as to be more closely connected with the final intended output?[10] (For example, can the performance of agencies concerned with arms control be more effectively evaluated by comparing the probability of destabilizing changes in an adversary's forces with and without a treaty, rather than by whether or not a treaty is signed?)

e. Can improved information, feedback, and evaluation systems be built into new policies and programs to reduce the risks of cooptation by a client group and to publicize it if it occurs? (For example, publicizing air traffic episodes and incidents in the vicinity of metropolitan airports would help passengers decide whether, when, and where to travel).

The normative questions of implementation analysis are no less formidable than those relating to the descriptive aspects discussed earlier. At best, attempts to respond systematically to the implementation questions raised by the nonmarket failure paradigm are likely to result in uncertain answers. Yet even without firm or complete answers, or indeed even without answers at all, there is merit in the exercise. Addressing the questions in specific policy contexts requires that they be reformulated with precise reference to those contexts. For each policy alternative, the cardinal implementation issues (who has to do what, when, how?) cannot be avoided. What has been omitted from virtually all policy studies, and what has significantly contributed to the failure of many implemented policies, must then be given explicit attention.

In sum, the premise of implementation analysis is that forewarned is forearmed. Knowing or being able to anticipate the types, sources, and mechanisms of nonmarket failures may help to mitigate, if not entirely to avoid, them, when moving from analysis and design to choice and implementation among public policy alternatives.

The analysis and anticipation of implementation problems shares a common objective with several other approaches to public policy analysis. For example, computerized simulations and manual or human "games" attempt to trace out the various consequences that may ensue from initially assumed conditions, when these conditions are complicated by the intervention of public policies, and by the choice of specific implementation actions by the participants. The various sources and types of nonmarket failure will tend to be manifest in the course of such simulations and games. Better and fuller anticipation of likely shortcomings can help to design measures, or suggest precautions, that can forestall the nonmarket failures. Some ineradicable minimum of nonmarket failure will remain.

But even if that remainder is still substantial, less is clearly better.

Notes

1. More than 90 percent of these are master's degrees. The RAND Graduate School and the Kennedy School at Harvard produce the largest numbers of doctorates in policy analysis—about eight annually (in 1992) at each institution.

2. Employment of the RAND Graduate School's Ph.D. recipients is divided about equally among government, the private commercial sector, and universities or private research organizations.

3. See Crecine (1981).

4. The term *missing chapter* was developed in conversations among Graham Allison, Andrew Marshall, and me to describe the usual neglect of implementation analysis in policy studies.

5. Summers (1965) and Harman (1971).

6. For a survey of this literature, see Hargrove (1975), Pressman and Wildavsky (1973), Allison (1974), and Derman (1978).

7. "If to do were as easy as to know what were good to do, chapels had been churches, and poor men's cottages princes' palaces. . . . I can easier teach twenty what were good to be done, than be one of the twenty to follow mine own teaching": William Shakespeare, *The Merchant of Venice*, Act 1, Scene II.

8. Some possible examples are (a) estimating the separate effect of noise emissions on property values in airport vicinities and obliging airlines to compensate property owners accordingly, while leaving to the airlines the choice of aircraft power plant, acoustical damping, or other measures to reduce noise; (b) using foreign trade policy as an adjunct or alternative to antitrust policy in maintaining competitive pressures in monopolistic industries; (c) reducing market imperfections (for example, by removing or lowering barriers to entry or providing adjustment assistance to facilitate factor mobility). See also chapter 8 for a discussion of ways in which government policies may sometimes contribute to improving and extending markets.

9. See Pascal et al. (1984), Neels and Caggiano (1984), Drucker (1969), Pascal (1972), and Rice (1975). The use of market analogues, incentives, and mechanisms to improve government performance is forcefully argued by Schultze (1977, 43–50, 55–62), and by Osborne and Gaebler (1992). See also chapter 8 for a discussion of ways in which market processes can be utilized to improve the functioning of government.

10. Such revisions are apt to involve consideration of agency personnel practices and in this respect would move implementation analysis in a direction taken by management consulting.

6 Comparing Market and Nonmarket Alternatives: General Considerations

Complexities in Comparing Markets and Nonmarkets

The existing theory of market failure provides a useful corrective to the theory of perfectly functioning markets. That theory, according to its advocates, leads to outcomes that are both efficient and, according to some criteria, socially equitable. Similarly, the theory of nonmarket failure outlined in the preceding chapters provides a corrective to the implicit theory of perfectly functioning governments. This theory, according to its supporters, also leads to efficient and equitable outcomes, or at least to ones that are more efficient and equitable than market outcomes.

In fact, and in contrast to the wishful images of their advocates, both markets and governments are prone to serious and predictable shortcomings described in preceding chapters.

Fair comparisons between market and nonmarket alternatives are extremely difficult to make. Because there is no generally applicable formula for choosing between them, the results of such comparisons often depend more on the predispositions of the evaluators than on their analyses.

In contemplating such comparisons, it is much easier to predict how specific types of market and nonmarket failures will affect the algebraic signs of outcomes—improving or worsening them—than to predict the size of these effects. For example, it is relatively easy to anticipate that the externalities of pollution, noise, and congestion generated by market activities are likely to be negative (that is, costs exceeding benefits), while the externalities resulting from public recreational facilities, parks (at least in the daytime), and police (at least most of the time) are likely to be positive (benefits exceeding costs). Estimating the size of these externalities is more difficult and can usually be ascertained only by detailed empirical work in specific cases and contexts. In practice, it is probably about as feasible to estimate the derived nonmarket externalities (negative as well as positive) resulting from environmental regulation as it is to estimate the market externalities (negative) resulting from unregulated strip mining, or from noise emissions near metropolitan airports.

The types and sources of market failure summarized in chapter 2 indicate the circumstances in which government intervention may be worth considering as countermeasures and alternative public policies worth analyzing as possible remedies. Similarly, the types and sources of nonmarket failure described in chapters 3 and 4 indicate the circumstances in which government intervention may itself misfire, whereupon a reevaluation of potential remedies—including possible reversion to a more nearly unfettered market, or to appropriately redesigned public policies ("counter-countermeasures")—may be necessary to avoid the actual or potential shortcomings of government intervention.

The complications involved in comparing market and nonmarket alternatives are formidable when the comparison is made in a static context; they become even more so when the comparison is attempted in a dynamic context— over an extended period, rather than at a point in time.

Several propositions, reasonably well grounded in fact or logic, suggest the complexities involved in this comparison.

Proposition 1: Subject to familiar and generally reasonable assumptions, efficient use of resources at any point in time requires that prices of outputs be equal to marginal costs.

If price exceeds marginal cost, efficiency will be enhanced by increasing output because the value of additional production, as reflected by its price, will be greater than the cost of producing it. When price falls short of marginal cost, efficiency will be enhanced by decreasing output because the value of additions to output will be less than their cost.

Consequently, an efficient economic system must be one that tends to conform to the rule of efficient pricing, while an inefficient system is one that does not.

Proposition 2: Many firms in market economies, including but not limited to the United States, frequently—and perhaps typically—do not set prices equal to marginal costs.

One reason for this is that firms often produce under conditions characterized by decreasing costs (increasing returns to scale). Where costs are decreasing, the costs of additional units of output (marginal costs) are less than average unit costs. Hence, firms producing under these conditions cannot set prices equal to marginal costs because they would not survive if they did—that is, they would not be able to cover their total costs if they priced at the cost of the marginal unit of output.

A second reason relates to market structure. Markets are often characterized by monopolistic competition, or are perceived by business management to be so characterized. In such imperfect markets, demand curves faced by firms are negatively sloping: sales can be increased only by reducing prices. These firms, whether they operate under conditions of decreasing or increasing costs, will therefore not set prices equal to marginal costs because profits are instead maximized at a higher price (and at a lower output).

The evidence in support of these two reasons for the frequent occurrence of inefficient pricing is debatable but strong enough to warrant serious consideration. In support of the pervasiveness of such imperfect markets is the frequent testimony of business managers that their products, including the services packaged and marketed with them, are differentiated from those of their competitors. They view their sales as occurring in submarkets with special links to particular customers and to particular geographic regions. Consequently, business managers view the demand curves they face as negatively sloping: demand increases as prices decline. Whether prices should be lowered depends not only on whether the lower price will cover the cost of additional output but also on whether the loss of revenue resulting from applying the lower price to the previous output level is made up by the increased sales volume.

Profits are therefore maximized at a higher price and at a lower output than the strict efficiency criterion of equality between marginal costs and prices would require. The profit-maximizing price may exceed or equal *average* costs, and profits may be supernormal or normal, respectively, depending on such factors as freedom of entry, labor union negotiating strategy, and, in Germany, the United Kingdom, and increasingly in the United States as well, labor/management practices in the areas of profit sharing, labor representation on corporate boards of directors (codetermination), and industrial democracy.

Empirical support for the first reason (decreasing costs) is admittedly arguable. The literature on economies of scale provides some evidence, although it is inconclusive.[1] Stronger supporting evidence can be found in the experience of practitioners in business, management consulting, and accounting. They tend to emphasize numerous sources of decreasing costs, such as pooling of overhead, including management, market research staff, legal services, accountants, labor relations specialists, and staff economists; widened span of control of central corporate decision makers (for example, in multinational corporations), relying on computerized management information systems with high initial costs; spreading of more or less fixed R&D costs, as well as marketing, advertising, and distribution costs, over a larger volume of output; and realizing pecuniary economies of scale from lowered input prices as a result of largescale purchases. As the list suggests, decreasing costs are viewed as growing both in their prevalence and in magnitude along with the progress of technology.

If decreasing costs are as prevalent (across industries, at least many of them—and over time, at least much of it) as this discussion suggests, what then limits the growth of industrial concentration? Why does the *largest* firm not become the *only* firm, simply because its costs are lowest and its competitive position therefore strongest?

One explanation is the relative inelasticity of firms' demand curves in such imperfect and fragmented submarkets. That is, further increases in sales can only be realized at prices proportionately lower than the relative increase in sales.

Political and legal institutions provide a second explanation. Even where demand is more elastic and responsive, firms may decide to limit output below the point at which their costs rise, because of existing antitrust regulation or, more frequently, because of the deterrent effects of anticipated antitrust litigation, or of possible legislative or administrative regulation. As a matter of business strategy, firms may choose to limit output rather than run the risks of antitrust litigation, legislative investigations, accusations of unfair competition from small business, investigative jour nalism, and the general harassment of consumerist and public interest pressures.

A final explanation is simply that decreasing costs may be less prevalent than is sometimes assumed. Beyond some scale of operations, diseconomies of scale may become dominant as a result of span-of-control limitations, the psychological as well as physical distance between management and labor, and possibly other deleterious effects of size on morale and productivity.[2]

In any event, firms that operate in the decreasing-cost region may adopt (for reasons of inelastic demand or for political-legal-strategic considerations), or have imposed upon them by regulatory bodies, average cost pricing, or marginal cost-plus-markup pricing, or some other pricing rule (for example, a fair rate of return). But they do not usually price at marginal cost.

Proposition 3: Nevertheless, it is now widely accepted (in general and among many who would accept propositions 1 and 2) that the market system and private enterprise are more efficient—both at a given point in time and especially over extended periods— than nonmarket systems (for example, centrally planned economies like that of the former Soviet Union) and nonmarket enterprises (for example, the large state enterprises in China), respectively.

As indicated earlier, the distinction between market and nonmarket organizations or systems can be defined simply. Market organizations derive their principal revenues from *prices* charged for output sold to consumers, who are free to buy or not to buy. Nonmarket organizations derive their principal revenues in other ways—for example, through taxes, appropriations, donations, and other nonprice sources.[3] Yet the distinction may not be quite so clear and simple in practice. Combinations are possible: nationalized firms or industries may charge prices but receive tax-supported subsidies to cover deficits; private firms may be subject to price controls and/or receive subsidies to cover costs or inflate profits; and some nonprofit institutions (such as RAND and various nonproprietary hospitals) are quasi-market organizations in that they derive most of their revenues by charging fees or prices to voluntary consumers.[4]

Hence, proposition 3 leads to a puzzle: How can market enterprises, which often do not practice the efficient pricing rule, be—or at least be considered—more efficient than nonmarket enterprises (such as public education and postal services), which do follow such a rule, or probably come closer to doing so?

This proposition concerning comparative efficiency has generally been supported by empirical work on the relative costs of public and private enterprises where both are producing comparable goods or services.[5] In their anthology of prior research on the subject, Borcherding and his colleagues found that private production was appreciably more efficient than public production in most fields where both were engaged (e.g., airlines, banking, bus services, fire protection, ocean tanker repair and maintenance, housing, hospitals), although not in all (e.g., efficiency comparisons in electric utilities and refuse collection showed mixed results, with public operation at lower cost in some instances and higher in others).[6]

Proposition 3 also derives support from observation of government operations at home and abroad, sometimes combined with a *gedanken* exercise of imagining how these operations would fare if performed by private enterprise.

At least two elements underlie these impressions. One is a widespread disenchantment with the efficiency of government operations in particular sectors (for example, in education and defense), as well as the pervasively inefficient performance of national economic systems in which the size of the public sector grew very rapidly, or became overwhelmingly dominant (the United Kingdom and the former Soviet Union, respectively).

The second element consists of a widespread belief—arising independently of the empirical work cited earlier—that in comparable fields private enterprise, which is exposed to the market, will generally and by a wide margin perform more efficiently than public enterprise, which is insulated from the market by subsidies, government protection and guarantees against losses, and assured sales. Examples that are consistent with this belief include the comparative performance of British Caledonian Airways and British Overseas Airways Corporation, state enterprise in China and private enterprises in the same industries in special economic zones within China and in Hong Kong and Taiwan, and the privately operated aerospace industry in the United States in relation to the nationalized (and subsidized) aerospace industry in Europe. This widespread belief does not derive from the empirical evidence cited above but instead from anecdotes and personal experiences suggesting that market organizations tend to be more efficient than nonmarket ones, while redundant costs tend to be associated with nonmarket organizations rather than market ones. Of course, both the belief and the empirical evidence relate to "private" goods without, or with few, externalities, as distinct from the market failure associated with the existence of public goods, and goods with significant externalities. In these latter cases, the resulting market failures may provide compelling arguments for the inadequacy of private market enterprises to produce socially efficient outputs by socially efficient processes, and the preferability of vesting responsibility in nonmarket organizations.

There is clearly a tension between propositions 1 and 2, on the one hand, and proposition 3 on the other. For all three propositions to be tenable, either one or both of the following conditions must apply:

a. Influences other than efficient pricing must operate to enhance the performance of the market system and outweigh its evident shortcomings in achieving allocative efficiency.

b. Nonmarket activities and regulations that attempt to rectify the market's own pricing inefficiencies must entail their own specific inefficiencies, and these must exceed the inefficiencies resulting from the market's own less-than-efficient pricing practices.

Condition (a) asserts that, although the market may not perform very well according to the rules of efficient (optimal) pricing, other sources of efficiency may nevertheless be associated with the market mechanism that redeem its economic performance. These other sources or types of efficiency, which I refer to as *nonpricing efficiencies*, may outweigh the market's shortcomings in regard to optimal pricing.

Condition (b) suggests that nonmarket activities (for example, government regulation or government production), while seeking to establish efficient pricing, may entail other sources of inefficiency that detract from the economic performance of these activities. These other sources or types of inefficiency, which I call *nonmarket inefficiencies*, may outweigh what nonmarket actions are able to accomplish in the domain of optimal pricing.

If neither nonpricing efficiencies nor nonmarket inefficiencies apply, then the case for the efficiency of the free market and market-governed enterprise is weakened, at least insofar as that case rests on the logic of economics.

If, on the other hand, either nonpricing efficiencies or nonmarket inefficiencies are of major significance, then the efficiency of the market system may be redeemed—but on grounds different from those on which microeconomics concentrates. In this case, the efficiency of the economics *discipline*, rather than the efficiency of markets, is brought into question: the elements on which economics primarily concentrates may not be those on which market efficiency primarily depends!

What are the nonpricing efficiencies and nonmarket inefficiencies that form the basis of the case for the market system and market enterprise? Partial answers are scattered through the literature on industrial organization and welfare economics, in the one case, and organization theory and behavior, in the other. They are not part of the central corpus of microeconomic theory, but instead are usually relegated to the penumbra of case studies and anecdotes.

There are three principal ingredients of nonpricing efficiencies: dynamic (or Schumpeterian) efficiency; technological (or "best-practice") efficiency; and X-efficiency.[7]

Dynamic efficiency is concerned with the ability of enterprises or economic systems to generate and sustain economic growth by developing new technology that lowers cost functions, improves product quality, or creates new and marketable products.

Technological efficiency is concerned with the ability of enterprises to search for and employ the best technology currently available, and hence to produce output at lower cost and/or of higher quality.

X-efficiency, as Leibenstein suggests, is concerned with the ability of enterprise management to lower costs and raise productivity for any given technology by organizational improvements, increased worker motivation, and better management practices. Many years ago the president of Sony remarked to me that, after careful disassembly and study of a wide range of American television equipment and examination of plant management methods, he had generally found it possible to lower American costs of production by 20 to 30 percent! The remark nicely captures elements of both technological and X-efficiency.

One can hypothesize that market enterprises perform better because they provide stronger incentives and greater rewards for all three types of nonpricing efficiency than do nonmarket enterprises and systems.

Alternatively, the analytical case for the market can be based on nonmarket inefficiencies—the argument that nonmarket production or regulatory activities tend to generate their own specific types of inefficiency, independent of their conformity to the optimal pricing rule.[8] The hypothesis can be advanced that predictable types of inefficiency are inherent in nonmarket activities (a contention that is central to the main thrust of this book). These nonmarket inefficiencies derive from the specific supply and demand characteristics, discussed in chapter 3, that are associated with the production and consumption of nonmarket output. As a consequence, nonmarket activities (for example, in the conduct of space or defense programs, or in the provision of regulatory services) often lead to redundant and increasing costs of production. Ancillary functions may be performed that contribute more to pleasing their producers (scientists, military officers, government administrators, etc.) than to accomplishing the purposes for which nonmarket activities were originally intended. As suggested in earlier chapters, the resulting pattern of nonmarket failure can be set against the existing theory of market failure as a counterpoint to the predictable departures of market outcomes from allocative efficiency.[9]

There is one general and neglected explanation that applies to both the evident inefficiencies of the nonmarket sector and the relative efficiency of the market sector. This explanation lies in the differing processes by which performance is monitored in the market and nonmarket domains.

Responsibility for monitoring nonmarket output usually is lodged in another public body: a cognizant legislative committee in the federal, state, or municipal legislature; a cognizant executive agency; or the General Accounting Office. The principal monitors are not consumers of output. Hence, the behavior of direct users—whether intended beneficiaries or inadvertent victims—does not typically impose any strict and regularized discipline on producers. A frustrated taxpayer may occasionally carp, or complain, or write to her (his) congressional representative, but the process by which this is translated into effective pressure toward efficient nonmarket production is sporadic and imprecise. Moreover, since nonmarket activities are typically carried out as exclusive "franchises," the discipline that might be exercised on nonmarket activities by competitive producers, pressing for an enlarged nonmarket share, is also absent.[10]

The resulting control over the costs and quality of nonmarket output is thus oblique and indirect, several steps removed from the production process, and therefore attenuated. In some cases where consumers of nonmarket output enter the process, they do so as self-appointed monitors, a subset of the consuming public with special interests that may be especially harmed (or helped) by the performance of a particular nonmarket activity—perhaps exemplified by the Sierra Club in relation to the maintenance of national parks and recreational areas. Frequently, consumers of nonmarket output have a keen interest in the quality of the product—for example, air traffic control, Coast Guard services, police—but little interest in the cost of production. As a result, oversight of nonmarket output by its consumers generally operates through ambiguous, uneven, and personalized political processes using such signaling and enforcement mechanisms as legislative hearings, lobbying, vote trading, floor amendments, and bargaining. Concern for more efficient nonmarket performance is usually not a principal motive and seldom a notable result of these mechanisms.

By contrast, in the market regime, control over performance is ultimately exercised by consumer behavior and by competing producers whose competition often occurs across product lines as well as within them. The process of controlling costs and quality impinges directly on market output, because the consumer can generally choose to buy less or shift to substitutes, while competing producers can expand their market shares by raising output, lowering prices, or adding to the substitutes that consumers can choose. The signaling and enforcement mechanism is more direct, impersonal, and evidently more effective.[11]

From the standpoint of marginal cost pricing, market regimes may often depart from the strict requirements of allocative efficiency. Yet operation of the market's feedback, signaling, and disciplining mechanism can compensate for this lapse by offsetting contributions to other types of efficiency—dynamic, technological, and X-efficiency. To be sure, firms operating in imperfectly competitive markets, and firms subject to decreasing costs, will not price their output at marginal cost. Yet their relative production costs will tend to be low, and their cost curves will tend to shift downward over time in response to market incentives. Moreover, their product quality and innovational propensities will generally be impressively high as a result of the stronger discipline and powerful incentives generated by the market than by the nonmarket.

By contrast, nonmarket activities may try to regulate or replace the allocative shortcomings of the market and may seek to get closer to an efficient pricing rule. The result may be the nonmarket inefficiencies referred to earlier: inflated total costs, a secular upward drift in cost functions, and changes in product quality to satisfy the professional or budgetary tastes of producers, rather than the demands of users or taxpayers.

Operation of the market sector's feedback mechanism accounts for the nonpricing efficiencies associated with that sector. And the occurrence of nonmarket inefficiencies is perhaps equally explained by the *absence* of this mechanism in the nonmarket sector.[12]

Noneconomic Dimensions of the Comparison

The complexities involved in comparing market and nonmarket alternatives increase still further if the evaluation criteria are widened to include noneconomic dimensions besides efficiency. The varying, and often conflicting, facets of distributional equity previously discussed provide one illustration of such added complexity. Some would argue, for example, that even in cases where a market solution is more efficient, the nonmarket (governmental) option is preferable because of the greater equity expected to be associated with it.

The other evaluation criteria sometimes mentioned in the literature are even less susceptible to quantitative measurement than is distributional equity: (1) *participation*—namely, the degree to which people, who are affected or are likely to be affected by a given choice between markets and governments, participate directly or indirectly in the planning and implementation of the choice; and (2) *accountability*—namely, the degree to which the outcome of a market or nonmarket choice is subject to a rigorous process of evaluation and postaudit concerning its effectiveness and acceptability.[13]

The classic illustration of participation as an evaluation criterion for choosing among nonmarket instruments is the New England town meeting or, at a more aggregative level, the populist, referendum-heavy California balloting process. The accountability criterion, as it applies to nonmarket or government instruments, ultimately depends on the democratic electoral process. Legislators and chief executives are, in the final analysis, accountable to their constituencies, or at least to 51 percent of their constituent voters. In practice, of course, such accountability typically depends on a much smaller subset of the constituency. With respect to any specific program or instrument or policy, a considerable part—usually most—of the aggregate constituency is generally passive. Hence, accountability reduces to a majority of the *subset* of the constituency actually interested in the specific program or issue, and this subset is often a small minority of the whole constituency.

By way of contrast, in the market context participation and accountability depend, respectively, on the anticipated and the actual (ex post) behavior of consumers who affect the emergence, expansion, or demise of a marketable product or service through their willingness to provide funds to sustain it. Participation in product development also depends, in the market context, on the wealth of potential investors who are willing to back it. The producer of marketed output is ultimately accountable to the purchasing power of consumers, while the producer of nonmarketed output is ultimately responsible to the voting power of concerned and active elements in the electorate. Accountability in the market sector may be diminished to the extent that producers exercise monopoly power, thereby limiting consumer choice. Accountability may also be diminished in the nonmarket sector to the extent that exclusivity of agency responsibility prevails. Thus, the Census Bureau is likely to be less responsive than the Postal Service.

In the nonmarket context, participation and accountability depend, respectively, on voice and vote. In the market context, participation and accountability depend, respectively, on wealth and purchases. Political campaigning and organizing are the nonmarket counterparts of promotion, marketing, and advertising in the market domain.

Comparisons between market and nonmarket alternatives, in terms of the participation and accountability criteria, are thus not only complex, but they are also likely to be
inconclusive, because the units of account—votes and purchasing power—are incommensurable. This consideration
suggests that comparisons involving participation and accountability may be more appropriate *within* the nonmarket
or government domain—that is, among the federal, state,
and local government levels—than *between* the nonmarket
and market alternatives. With respect to the performance of
public welfare transfers and services—a presumptively nonmarket function or activity—higher levels of government
(that is, federal or state government) seem to perform more
satisfactorily than lower levels in regard to the accountability criterion, while local governments—municipalities,
townships, and counties—perform more effectively than
higher ones in regard to the participation criterion: participation tends to decline as jurisdictional size increases, while
the public's evaluation and effective influence (accountability) tends to improve at higher jurisdictional levels.[14]

Within the nonmarket domain, the comparison and
choice among different levels of government to perform
particular functions and exercise particular responsibilities
may heavily depend on prevailing public attitudes toward
these government levels, precisely because the criteria of
participation and accountability are so elusive. In this connection, it is worth noting that public opinion polling by
the Advisory Commission on Intergovernmental Relations
showed, between 1972 and 1981, a 30 percent decline in the
proportion of respondents providing a favorable evaluation
of the federal government, while favorable evaluation of
state and local government recorded increases of 39 percent
and 27 percent, respectively.[15] In a 1991 survey conducted
by the Gallup organization, four times as many respondents
judged that state and local government spend their "tax

dollars most wisely" as judged that the federal government does so.[16]

Although the criteria of participation and accountability thus seem generally to be more applicable to performance comparisons among alternative levels of government than to comparisons between market and nonmarket alternatives, instances occasionally arise in which these criteria are quite strikingly applicable in the market context as well. One such example relates to the much-heralded introduction by the Coca-Cola Company in 1985 of a new, sweeter beverage as part of its enduring competition for market share with Pepsi-Cola. The effect of this new version of the classic Coca-Cola taste was a surprisingly intense and negative response from a vocal segment of Coca-Cola's established customer base. A voluminous outpouring of letters, telephone calls, and public reaction ensued, causing the company's top management to change its strategy by restoring to the market its prior Coca-Cola formula as a second product dubbed "Coke Classic." Moreover, the backtracking occurred well in advance of the usual indicators of sales, shares, and profits. The process was, in many respects, more akin to the "voice and vote" process associated with the nonmarket than to the "wealth and purchases" mechanism characterizing the market.

In effect, this was an instance where Coca-Cola's management was weighed in the balance and found wanting by an important part of its constituency. Management was, in fact, more accountable than one might have expected, or than the management itself expected.

This incident, and the ensuing reinstatement of the established "Classic" product, provides a striking demonstration in the market sphere of participation by the consuming public and accountability to it by corporate management. The analogue of "voice and vote" in the market sphere appeared, in the nonmarket sphere, as a vocal threat to buy Pepsi!

In both the market and government contexts, accountability depends on relatively large groups: voters in the governmental context and consumers in the market context. The political process, on which governmental accountability principally depends, typically involves relatively well-organized interest groups, rather than a majority of the voters. Such groups are especially concerned with a particular piece of legislation, or a nonmarket service, such as health or welfare or education, or the regulatory activities of nonmarket agencies. Each of these respective nonmarket outputs tends, then, to be accountable to the interest group, rather than to the voting majority of the public at large.

In the market context, producers are, and tend to view themselves as, accountable to current and potential consumers of their product line. However, in this case, too, especially concerned and organized groups or subgroups—such as those represented by Ralph Nader, Common Cause, and the development of consumerism in recent decades—frequently exercise an influence on the behavior of producers disproportionate to the size of the subgroup itself. Access to the media by such subgroups always entails a risk to producers operating in a competitive market: vocal reactions, though initially confined to a relatively small group of the consuming public, might be transmitted to a considerably larger group, thereby eroding the producers' market share and profitability.

Accountability to individual citizens in the governmental context, and to individual consumers in the market context, is generally and properly limited. Producers of market output are concerned with individual consumers only, or principally, to the extent that the individual consumer may be representative of the larger consuming public. Correspondingly, producers of nonmarket output tend to be concerned with the reactions of individual citizens only to the extent that those reactions are viewed as potentially representative of the reactions of a larger group of the voting public.

Thus, there are some similarities between the accountability of producers of nonmarket output and that of producers of market output: accountability in the nonmarket context occurs through the political process and the behavior of voters; accountability in the market context occurs through the competitive market process and the behavior of consumers. This characterization relates to "macroaccountability"—that is, accountability, in the large, of the nonmarket and market producers, respectively. What might be termed "microaccountability" describes the responsiveness and responsibility of nonmarket and market producers, respectively, to the reactions, concerns, and complaints of individual citizens and consumers. Microaccountability is particularly hard to measure and therefore hard to evaluate. At the micro level, one has to rely on personal experience in comparing the responsiveness of governmental agencies and bureaucratic processes to the concerns and complaints of individuals with the speed and adequacy of response by automobile producers, airlines, and soft drink manufacturers (e.g., Coca-Cola in the episode referred to above) to the concerns and complaints of individual consumers.

Notes

1. See, for example, Scherer (1970), Moore (1959), Hall and Weiss (1967), Bain (1956), and Haldi and Whitcomb (1967).

2. Some of the management literature stresses certain advantages—closer contact and rapport between management and labor, participation, communication, knowing the customer as well as the plant, and "management by walking around"—that are more difficult to realize as scale increases. See, for example, Peters and Austin (1985).

3. See Bacon and Eltis (1976) and Wolf (1979a).

4. See the discussion of nonprofit organizations in chapter 4.

5. See Osborne and Gaebler (1992) and the summary provided in appendix B.

6. See Borcherding, Pommerehne, and Schneider (1982) and the further discussion in chapter 7.

7. The existence and importance of these sources and types of efficiency have, of course, been well recognized in economics outside the realm of comparative statics. See, for example, Schumpeter (1934), Weintraub (1949, 202–203, 406–407), Leibenstein (1966), and Nicholson (1972, 306–307).

8. The clearest examples, of course, relate to nonmarket activities that charge low or no prices and have low, if not zero, marginal costs, such as education, postal services and, in a special sense, genuine public goods such as defense and space programs.

9. See chapters 3 and 4.

10. See chapter 3.

11. Of course, the signals can be weakened and the enforcement mechanism nullified where, as in the former Soviet economy and that of China apart from its dynamic, marketized coastal economic zones, a seller's market for consumers' goods usually prevails, as an intended or inadvertent result of centralized control over production and wages.

12. Newhouse's study of the health care industry provides an interesting example of the power and effectiveness of this mechanism. Costs and prices have risen faster and farther in those parts of the industry for which coinsurance coverage of consumer costs is higher (e.g., hospital services) than in those parts for which coinsurance is lower (e.g., dental services and drugs). Insurance insulates producers of hospital services from the signaling and enforcement mechanism of the market because it reduces the consumer's incentive to search for efficient suppliers. See Newhouse (1970).

13. See Ross (1984, 12–19).

14. Ibid., 55ff.

15. See Advisory Commission on Intergovernmental Relations (1981).

16. See Roper Center for Public Opinion Research (1991).

7

Comparing Market and Nonmarket Alternatives: Empirical Aspects

The Power and the Pitfalls of Quantitative Comparisons

Because efficiency is the most measurable of the several performance criteria previously discussed, there is an understandable tendency to emphasize it in comparisons between the performance of the market and the nonmarket. This emphasis brings to mind the parable of looking for the key where the light is, rather than where the key fell. An uncharitable, but not wholly inaccurate, critic might say that modern social science in general, and economics in particular, tends to be more concerned with what is measurable and quantifiable than with what is important and relevant.

While acknowledging that there is some merit to this criticism, one can effectively answer it without making excessive claims about the advantages of quantification. The choice between market and nonmarket alternatives and various possible combinations between them will, and often should, entail important, and sometimes overriding, qualitative judgments relating to the less measurable criteria of equity, participation, and accountability. Nevertheless, these qualitative judgments themselves can be greatly helped and focused by a clearer appreciation of whether efficiency gains or losses are associated with one choice or another, and if so, how large they are, and with which choice they're associated.

For example, even if option A seems preferable to option B on grounds of equity or participation or accountability, it is usually important in the decision-making process to inquire about the size of the efficiency losses likely to be incurred by selecting one option over the other. In those rare cases where pure dominance exists between or among the alternatives, the answer is none; that is, option A is not only preferable to option B on the qualitative grounds of equity or participation but at the same time does not involve any efficiency losses compared with option B.

However, trade-offs more typically occur among these dimensions. For example, raising the level of direct social welfare payments, or providing for direct payments to low-income recipients through a negative income tax, may seem socially desirable on grounds of equity. But, if the first of these options reduces labor supply by, say, 3 percent, while the second option reduces it by only 1 percent, then the second may be a preferable policy for achieving a desired change in income distribution. Even if social or environmental rather than efficiency considerations provide the basis for maintaining rather than closing a military base at one location or another, or for awarding a procurement contract to one bidder or another, it still is important to know whether the efficiency losses incurred by acting on these considerations are small or large compared with the results of basing the choice on efficiency grounds alone.

So, the size of the efficiency loss or gain matters even where the burden of choice rests heavily on qualitative, social, and judgmental grounds.

In sum, one can strongly and convincingly argue for the importance of efficiency gains and losses in comparing alternative policies or actions, provided one avoids the pitfall of presuming or pretending that these considerations are or should be the exclusive or the predominant basis for choosing among the alternatives. Conversely, in urging that particular alternatives are to be preferred on grounds other than the possible efficiency gains or losses associated with them, one need not ignore the importance of calculating the relevant gains and losses.

Micro and Macro Comparisons

The previously cited work by Borcherding, Pommerehne, and Schneider summarized the results of fifty empirical studies relating mainly to microeconomic efficiency: allocative efficiency in particular fields of production or service delivery. The Borcherding survey focused principally on comparisons between private and public output (federal, state, and local) in the United States, Germany, Switzerland, Australia, and Canada in terms of their relative production efficiency (i.e., the costs of delivering more or less homogeneous units of product or service) in nineteen fields of activity: airlines; banks; bus services; cleaning services; debt collection; electric utilities; fire protection; forestry; hospitals; housing; insurance claims processing; insurance sales and servicing; ocean tanker repair and maintenance; railroads; refuse collection; savings and loans; slaughterhouses; water utilities; and weather forecasting.[1]

In forty of the fifty case studies that were reviewed, private (that is, market) supply was more efficient than public (nonmarket) supply. In three studies (having to do with electric utilities, veterans' hospitals, and garbage collection), nonmarket provision appeared to be less costly than market delivery. In five studies (dealing with Canadian railroads, refuse collection in St. Louis and Minneapolis, electric utilities in various parts of the United States, and insurance sales and servicing in West Germany), the results showed no difference between public and private production efficiency, while in two of the studies the results were too ambiguous to permit any conclusions to be drawn. Appendix B reproduces a tabular summary of the survey done by Borcherding and his colleagues, as well as more recent surveys by Osborne and Gaebler (1992) and by Fitzgerald (1988), comparing public and private service delivery in health care, transportation, refuse collection, aircraft repair, and environmental protection.

Other studies have produced similar results. For example, the Chief Administrative Officer of Los Angeles County reported that the county's program of shifting to private contractors functions previously performed by county agencies resulted in annual savings in 1985 of 35 percent. The Los Angeles privatization program—covering health services, facilities management, data processing, parks and recreation, public social services, and other functions—entailed annual contracts of $43 million for services that were estimated to cost $66 million if provided by county agencies.[2]

Another analysis completed in 1984 for the Department of Housing and Urban Development found that the cost of street construction by city agencies was 96 percent greater than similar work done by private contractors, 43 percent greater for street cleaning, 73 percent for janitorial services, 56 percent for traffic-signal maintenance, and 37 percent for tree pruning. In each case the analysis controlled for differences in the quality of service.[3]

Still another example is provided by an analysis of 235 contracts awarded by the Department of Defense in fiscal years 1981 and 1982. According to the Office of Management and Budget (OMB), the cost of contractor operation was 24 percent less than the bids submitted by the in-house work force, which, on average, had already reduced their costs by 7 percent. Thus, OMB's Office of Federal Procurement Policy concluded that "the overall savings resulting from the competitive process were in excess of 30 percent."[4]

A 1988 study, originally undertaken as a RAND Graduate School doctoral dissertation by Randy Ross, presented public-private sector comparisons that are somewhat more mixed and complex than those referred to in the previously cited studies. Ross compared performance in the public and private sectors in three fields—electric power, mental health, and school bus transportation. He found that the public sector evidently distributes electricity more efficiently than either regulated or unregulated private firms, for reasons that he suggested may relate to the quality of public sector management in this field, to overcapitalization of regulated private firms, or to the higher sales and advertising costs incurred by private firms. By contrast, in the field of mental health, he found that both the production and insurance functions are performed more efficiently by the private sector than by government, although he suggested that equity, participation, and accountability considerations may warrant the assumption in this area of responsibilities by the public sector.

Finally, in school bus transportation, Ross found that, while private sector operations are more efficient, institutional arrangements that involve a combination of public and private sector operations performed nearly as well as private operations alone. Evidently, the existence of active private transportation operations acts as a spur to efficiency for public school operators that does not exist in the absence of such competition.[5]

As previously noted, the studies surveyed by Borcherding and his colleagues, as well as the other comparative studies referred to earlier, focused on what I have called microeconomic efficiency—namely, the input costs of delivering or producing a particular service or product at a given point in time. A different approach to comparing market and nonmarket outcomes is represented by empirical work done by Keith Marsden at the World Bank, and also by the author at RAND, dealing with what I shall call macroeconomic efficiency. Where the Borcherding survey focused on particular sectors or industries within different national economies at a point in time, the macroeconomic work dealt with comparisons among countries in terms of their respective rates of growth over time. The Borcherding survey focused on allocative efficiency, while the work done by Marsden and by RAND dealt with dynamic efficiency.[6]

One of the difficult problems in macroeconomic comparisons among countries, with respect to the distinction between the market and the nonmarket, is the choice of an appropriate scale for measuring the relative size of the market and nonmarket sectors. Marsden's work focused on the relation between taxes and economic performance, while the RAND work focused on government spending as well as tax revenues as indicators of the relative size of the nonmarket sector. Both of these metrics—taxes and government spending—are, at best, proxies for measuring the size and scope of the nonmarket sector. Government spending may be a preferable indicator because it is more inclusive: since most national budgets tend to be in deficit much more often than they are in balance or in surplus, government spending will include, but will usually exceed, tax revenues.

Nevertheless, both spending and taxes may err in accurately conveying the scope of nonmarket activity and government intervention. For example, government spending as a fraction of gross domestic product in 1989 was only slightly less in Germany (46 percent) than in France (49 percent),[7] but the French economy is much more *dirigiste*—that is, subject to nonmarket control and influence—than is the more competitive, market-oriented economy of Germany. Similarly, the share of GDP represented by government spending in 1989 in South Korea (17 percent) was about the same as that in India (18 percent), although the role and vitality of the market sector is manifestly greater in Korea than in India.[8]

The point is that the extent of nonmarket intervention or control is only partially indicated by government tax revenues or government spending. Government regulatory, legislative, and bureaucratic interventions may be extensive or limited, although neither government spending nor tax revenue may accurately reflect the role and rule of the nonmarket.[9] Also, in the national accounts of different countries, figures for government spending often include varying proportions of transfer payments, instead of uniformly reflecting only or principally value-added by the nonmarket sector to the national product. Nevertheless, such transfer payments have relevance to the market-nonmarket distinction because they suggest one aspect of the nonmarket's influence over the market sector.

Marsden's empirical work is based on an ingenious sample of ten paired countries covering the period 1970–1979. The members of each pair had approximately the same per capita income level but sharply different ratios between tax revenues and GNP. Thus, each of the ten pairs includes a low-tax and a high-tax country, with annual per capita income levels varying between $200 and $300, and $8,800 and $12,000 in 1979 dollars, for the ten pairs in the group.[10]

Marsden regressed the real average annual growth rate in the 1970s of each of the twenty countries on its corresponding ratio of tax revenues to gross domestic product. This ratio, as noted earlier, is a relevant, if imperfect, indicator of the actual scale and extent of the nonmarket sector. Marsden's main result is a statistically significant *negative* relationship between growth rates and tax shares: on the average, for the sample as a whole, for each 1 percent increase in the ratio of tax revenues to gross domestic product, real annual growth decreases by 0.36 percent. Furthermore, nearly 45 percent of the variation in average annual growth rates across the sample of twenty countries is explained by variations in the ratios of their respective taxes

Table 7.1
Regression analysis of Economic Growth and Tax Revenues for Selected
Countries, 1970–1979

Regression equation	Number of observations	Regression coefficients for ratio of tax revenues to GNP	Constant	Coefficient of determination (R^2)
Total sample	20	−0.36 (−3.80)	11.3	.45
Lower-income countries	10	−0.58 (−3.90)	13.9	.66
Higher-income countries	10	−0.34 (−2.90)	11.8	.52

Source: Keith Marsden, *Links between Taxes and Economic Growth: Some Empirical Evidence*, World Bank Staff Working Paper 605, Washington, D.C., 1983.
a. Economic growth is measured as average annual rate of change in real gross domestic product for the 1970–1979 period. T-statistics are shown in parentheses.

to their gross domestic products.[11] Marsden's principal results are summarized in table 7.1.

Recalling our earlier discussion of distributional equity as one criterion for comparing market and nonmarket outcomes, Marsden also finds that the connection between high growth and low relative tax revenues does not appear to be at the expense of equity of income distribution in the low-tax/high-growth countries; nor does it appear to be at the expense of consumption growth, improvements in government services, or increases in social welfare (as reflected by changes in infant mortality and life expectancy) in countries at the same paired levels of per capita income.[12]

While Marsden's work is important and relevant, several qualifications should be borne in mind in interpreting his results.

First, data dealing with international income comparisons in dollar terms, and international comparisons of growth rates, should be treated with caution, as Marsden himself plainly points out. The use of a dollar standard for countries with differing economic structures, different relative prices, differing involvement in international trade, and differing degrees of exchange rate overvaluation can lead to questionable results. Second, while the data sources that he uses are the best available, this is a field in which the best are none too good. Finally, national economic performance—especially in the less-developed countries—surely depends on many other factors besides tax revenues, or the relative size of the market and the nonmarket sectors. For example, economic growth depends critically on political stability and on education, training, and the quality of the labor force. It also is influenced by monetary policy, foreign exchange policy, and trade policies. Clearly, these important policy dimensions are not reflected in either the tax ratio as a measure of the size of the nonmarket sector or in the government spending measure used in the RAND work to be discussed.

Like the World Bank study, the empirical work done at RAND focused on international and intertemporal economic performance.[13] The metric for evaluating performance, like that used by Marsden, is annual rates of growth in real GDP. The principal differences between the RAND work and Marsden's work are the following:

1. The RAND sample is somewhat larger—twenty-seven countries, rather than twenty. The countries we selected were chosen principally according to the availability of reasonably reliable and comparable data for those in the sample, rather than by the paired sampling method employed in Marsden's work. Countries in our sample span a wide range of per capita income levels and levels of development, but we have not performed the careful matching of countries at the same income levels as in Marsden's study.

2. Our sample includes thirteen upper-income countries (Australia, Belgium, Denmark, Finland, France, Ireland,

Norway, Spain, Sweden, Switzerland, the United Kingdom, the United States, and West Germany); nine middle-income countries (Argentina, Brazil, Chile, Costa Rica, the Dominican Republic, Mexico, Paraguay, South Korea, and Tunisia); and five low-income countries (Indonesia, Kenya, Malawi, Thailand, and Zaire).[14] In this sample, the range of per capita income extends from less than $1,300 per year for the low-income group, to between $1,300 and $2,600 for the middle-income countries, and above $2,600 for the upper-income countries.

3. The original RAND study covered the period 1972–1982, Marsden's 1970–1979. The RAND work has been updated to cover the 1983–1987 period, as well.

4. We have employed both total government spending and tax revenues as independent variables in the regression analysis, compared with Marsden's use of tax revenues alone. In both cases, government spending and the tax variables are expressed as a fraction of gross domestic product.

It is interesting to note that the correlation between gross aggregate government spending and tax revenues for the twenty-seven countries in the sample is high, 0.96, for the 1972–1982 period, and 0.93 for the 1983–1987 years, so the results should not be very different on this count. From the standpoint of the focus on markets and governments in this book, use of aggregate government spending is probably preferable to tax revenues as an indicator of the size and scope of government. Aggregate government spending exceeds tax revenues by the amount of government borrowing to cover budget deficits. Government spending also covers the costs of direct government employment and production as well as transfer payments and subsidies and other categories of nonpurchase activities of government, such as foreign aid, interest on the public debt, and civil service and military pensions. All of these types of expenditure reflect, albeit imperfectly, the relative scope of non-market activities.

As noted earlier, there is no single measure that accurately reflects the scope of the nonmarket sector—because of regulatory and legislative interventions that may be larger or smaller in different countries, but that are not conveyed by either tax yields or government spending. Nevertheless, total government spending is a more comprehensive indicator of the scope of the nonmarket sector than is tax revenue. Since our focus is the comparison between governments and markets, and between nonmarket and market failure as impediments to efficient, equitable, accountable, and participatory performance, aggregate spending seems to be more suitable for the purpose at hand.

The principal results of the RAND work are summarized in table 7.2 and figure 7.1.

As indicated in table 7.2 for the all-country sample for the 1972–1982 years, there are statistically significant nega-

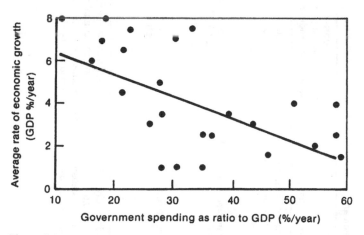

Figure 7.1
Government spending and economic growth

Table 7.2
Regression analysis of economic growth, government spending, and tax revenues for selected countries, 1972–1982[a]

Regression equation	Number of observations	Regression coefficients for ratio of government expenditure to GDP	Regression coefficients for ratio of tax revenue to GDP	Constant	Coefficient of determination R^2 (adjusted)
All countries in sample (OECD, middle-income, low-income)	27	-.10 (-3.40)	—	7.38	.32
	27	—	-.11 (-2.90)	6.79	.25
Middle-income and OECD countries	22	-.09 (-2.90)	—	6.99	.30
	22	—	-.11 (-2.90)	6.96	.29
Low-income countries	5	-.43 (-3.80)	—	16.01	.77[b]
	3	—	-.32 (-.60)	9.98	.12

Source: International Monetary Fund, *International Financial Statistics*, 1984, and *Government Financial Statistics Yearbook*, 1984.
a. Economic growth is measured as the average annual percentage change in real gross domestic product over the 1972–1982 period. T-statistics are shown in parentheses.
b. R^2 has been adjusted to allow for small sample size.

tive relationships between central government expenditures or tax revenues as percentages of GDP and average annual growth. On the average, a 10 percent increase in the ratio of government spending to GDP results in an expected decrease of 1 percent in the average annual rate of growth in GDP. Similarly, a 10 percent increase in the ratio of tax revenues to GDP results in an expected decrease of 1.1 percent in average annual growth in GDP. For the low-income countries, the relationship is also statistically significant, but the regression coefficients are substantially higher: for each increase of 10 percent in the ratio of government spending to GDP, the relationship suggests an expected decrease of 4 percent in the average annual rate of growth. Figure 7.1 shows the fitted regression of economic growth rates on government spending shares and, separately, on tax revenue shares.

The results are similar for the 1983–1987 period. Again, for the all-country and middle-income countries in the sample, the regression coefficients show a statistically significant negative relationship between the average GDP growth rate and the ratio of government spending to GDP, and between GDP growth and the tax revenue ratio. Table 7.3 summarizes the 1983–1987 results.[15]

A number of caveats and cautionary comments, similar to those mentioned concerning Marsden's results, should be made regarding the interpretation of these results. First, the data used in these intercountry and intertemporal regressions leave much to be desired; hence, the results should be considered as suggestive, rather than conclusive.

Second, both the RAND and World Bank results are based on extremely simple models that make no allowance for intercountry differences in the extent of government regulation; in monetary, fiscal, foreign exchange, and commercial policies; in technology; in the capital stock; in the quality of the labor force; or in prevailing conditions of political stability and security. Marsden's work allows for differences

Table 7.3
Regression analysis of economic growth, government spending, and tax revenues for selected countries, 1983–1987

Regression equation	Number of observations	Regression coefficients for ratio of government expenditure to GDP	Regression coefficients for ratio of tax revenue to GDP	Constant	Coefficient of determination R^2 (adjusted)
All countries in sample	26*	-.10 (-2.00)	—	.07	.10
	27	—	-.15 (-2.70)	.08	.19
Middle-income and OECD countries	22	-.09 (-1.70)	—	.09	.08
	22	—	-.16 (-2.50)	.08	.19
Low-income countries	4*	-.35 (-11.10)	—	.14	.98
	5	—	-.07 (-.30)	.07	-.30

Source: International Monetary Fund, *Government Financial Statistics Yearbook*, 1991.
*Government expenditures for Zaire are unavailable.

in per capita income levels by the pairing of countries with approximately equal levels, as described earlier; the RAND work does not make such an allowance. (Actually, a priori arguments can be made on both sides of the question whether higher income countries will grow faster or slower than lower income ones, so omission of the per capita income variable from the model, in a mixed sample of high-, middle-, and low-income countries, may not sacrifice much in explanatory power.)

Third, in light of the sparseness of the RAND model, it is not surprising that only a moderate proportion of the intercountry variation in growth rates is explained by the variation in the relative share of government spending in the countries included in the sample: 32 percent of the variance in the all-country sample; 30 percent for the OECD and middle-income countries; and 77 percent for the low-income countries. And these explanatory proportions for the 1972–1982 years are appreciably reduced for the OECD and middle-income countries in the 1983–1987 period. Much of the intercountry growth variance must be attributable to the other factors mentioned earlier, apart from the effect of the nonmarket sector's size as reflected by government spending.[16] (Indeed, it is more surprising that this simple model explains such a high proportion of the variance than that the proportion is not higher.)

Finally, it should be noted that the relationships described in both the RAND and World Bank work are a matter of continuing study as well as continuing controversy. For example, Mancur Olson's study of long-term secular growth finds no reliable connection between the size of government and economic growth, although he acknowledges a small inverse relation since the 1970s.[17] Frederic Pryor's comparison of growth rates in the OECD and the CMEA (Council for Mutual Economic Assistance) countries of Eastern Europe finds no difference between their respective real growth rates in the 1950–1980 period, after allowing for other explanatory factors besides the systemic difference in the role of government.[18]

By way of contrast to Pryor's results, Daniel Landau's study of the relationship between government consumption expenditures and per capita economic growth for the 1961–1976 period shows results similar to those reached by RAND and the World Bank.[19]

Nevertheless, as a rough measure of dynamic efficiency in the performance of economic systems, the results of the RAND work and the Marsden work are consistent, mutually reinforcing, and significant. Notwithstanding the fact that many other influences are at work—some under the control of individual countries and their policies, and others, such as oil prices and international terms of trade, largely beyond their control—in general and on the average, a larger and growing nonmarket sector tends to be associated with a lower rate of economic growth. As noted earlier, economic growth is not the only important consideration to be taken into account in evaluating economic and social systems. However, it is surely one important dimension relevant to the cardinal choice concerning the desirable scope of government and the market.

Notes

1. See Borcherding, Pommerehne, and Schneider (1982).

2. Memorandum from James C. Hankla, Chief Administrative Officer, Los Angeles County, to County Board of Supervisors, *Report on Board Awarded Contracts*, August 2, 1985.

3. See Stevens (1984). I am indebted to E. S. Savas for this reference, as well as the succeeding one.

4. Office of Management and Budget (1984).

5. This case provides support for our previous consideration of the cost-inflating effects of exclusivity in nonmarket supply. See Ross (1988).

6. See Marsden (1983).

7. See OECD (1992). The fraction shown for Germany in 1989 probably rose after unification of East and West Germany in 1990.

8. International Monetary Fund (1991).

9. For a similar view, see Schmidt in Forte and Peacock (1985).

10. See Marsden (1983, table 2, p. 3). Marsden's ten pairs of countries, in ascending order of per capita income, are Malawi (low tax), Zaire (high tax); Cameroon (low tax), Liberia (high tax); Thailand, Zambia; Paraguay, Peru; Mauritius, Jamaica; South Korea, Chile; Brazil, Uruguay; Singapore, New Zealand; Spain, the United Kingdom; and Japan, Sweden.

11. Ibid., 10.

12. Ibid., 4–5ff. Marsden evaluated the equity of income distribution in terms of the share of total income received by the poorest 40 percent of households.

13. This work has been done by the author and Randy Ross, a former graduate fellow in The RAND Graduate School.

14. Both the RAND and Marsden samples omitted countries heavily dependent on oil exports, with the single exception of the United Kingdom.

15. For the low-income countries, table 7.3 indicates a significantly negative relation between the government spending ratio and average GNP growth but none between the tax ratio and GNP growth. This surprising result is due to the relatively low correlation (0.71) between tax revenues ratios and government spending ratios for the low-income countries in the 1983–1987 period.

16. The relatively modest R^2s are not surprising for another reason as well. In general, lower-income LDCs—some of which are included in the sample—typically have low ratios of government spending to GDP because of the relatively high share of their output characteristically provided by the rural agricultural sector, which is often remote from government. Interestingly, this structural difference tends to lower the R^2s that result from the pooled sample compared with the low-income sample alone.

17. Pryor (1985). Actually, Pryor's systemic dummy variable shows a *negative* effect of the CMEA, centrally planned systems, which is consistent with the results obtained by RAND and Marsden. How-

ever, the corresponding coefficient in the systemic dummy variable is only significant at a 15 percent level. See his table 2 (1985, 213). Pryor's model specification, which includes per capita GDP as an independent variable, may also obscure some of the effect of the systemic dummy.

18. Olson (1982).

19. Landau (1983).

8

Conclusions: The Choice between Markets and Governments

Guidelines for Choice

The choice between markets and governments is complex, and it is usually not binary. Rather than being a pure choice between markets *or* governments, it is usually a choice between different combinations of the two, and different degrees of one or another mode of allocating resources. If the preferred and predominant choice is in favor of the market, a significant role for the nonmarket (that is, government) will and, for reasons relating to the pervasiveness and inevitability of market failures, *should* remain. This role relates especially to the production of pure public goods, such as defense and national security, to establishing and maintaining the legal and other environmental conditions that are essential for the functioning of markets, and to the provision of the necessary redistributive services and programs that constitute an acceptable safety net for society and that reflect the standards of "distributive justice" with which that society is, as Viner put it, "tolerably content."[1]

If, on the other hand, the preferred and predominant choice is in favor of allocative decision making by nonmarket means (that is, by government), a significant role for the market may and, for reasons relating to the pervasiveness and inevitability of nonmarket failure, *should* also remain.

Even in highly centralized systems, such as that of China and the former Soviet Union and some of its successor republics, market activity will arise, either as underground or second economy transactions where government policy is severely restrictive, or as open transactions responding to market-based incentives where government policy (as in China) is more permissive. Quite apart from the norms and intentions of the leadership, the incentives created by centralized, nonmarket-regulated activities will lead to evasion, black or gray markets, and under-the-table, quasi-market behavior. Indeed, the experience in the late 1980s of Eastern Europe and the Soviet Union, until its dissolution in 1992, suggests that the tendency toward market encroachment on allocation by government is stronger than the presumption that was advanced in the 1950s and 1960s of an inevitable historical trend in the opposite direction.

Consequently, neither Milton Friedman nor Kenneth Galbraith finds, or is likely to find, the prevailing scale of market and nonmarket activities in the United States congenial to his tastes and preferences, even though the predominant choice tends toward the market. Similarly, neither committed market-oriented reformers like Larisa Piyasheva, nor advocates of a predominant state sector like Evgeny Yasin, finds or is likely to find the prevailing scale of nonmarket and market activities in Russia to be congenial to their respective tastes and preferences.

While the choice between markets and governments is thus a matter of emphasis and degree, these differences matter enormously in their effects on the performance, as well as the fairness, of economic and social systems. To help illuminate this choice, several guiding propositions can be distilled from the preceding discussion.

In considering the resulting distillate, the reader should be reminded that my aim in the previous chapters has not been to give equal time to consideration of the shortcomings of markets and nonmarkets. Instead, the aim has been deliberately to emphasize nonmarket failures on the premise that the dissection of market failures has previously received ample and rigorous treatment in the existing literature, while those of the nonmarket have not been similarly analyzed.

Static and Dynamic Efficiency

As a general allocative mechanism, markets do a better job than governments, from the standpoint of both allocative (or static) efficiency (namely, realizing a higher ratio between outputs or product, on the one hand, and inputs or costs, on the other) and dynamic efficiency (namely, sustaining a higher rate of economic growth over time). Market systems tend to be more efficient in the use of resources at a given point in time and more innovative, dynamic, and expansive over time. Generally, the sources and types of nonmarket failure outweigh the not insubstantial ones associated with market failure, at a given point in time and in the short run. Over longer periods, the deviation of market regimes from optimal pricing practices is outweighed by the nonpricing efficiencies generated by market incentives and competition.

Several qualifications, most of which have been explicitly or implicitly referred to in the preceding discussion, should be added to the foregoing conclusion.

First, this proposition assumes that production of pure public goods—such as defense and public order—is maintained by government. Under a market regime, market failure would inevitably result in deficient output of such public goods, because of their inherent "publicness."

Second, there is no formula for establishing the essential minimum threshold of government activities and outputs beyond which the proposition about the relative merits of the market over the nonmarket applies. For example, the proposition does not imply that, if government attains a level of 30 percent of a nation's GNP, the economy as a whole will be less efficient—both allocatively and dynamically—than if the government sector is only 28 percent.

Moreover, there is no simple or agreed-upon metric for precisely measuring the size of the nonmarket. Government spending as a share of GNP might be small, but the regulatory, administrative, and legal interventions and controls exercised by government might nonetheless make the effective reach of the nonmarket sector extremely wide. Conversely, the government sector might be relatively large as a share of GNP, yet many government activities might themselves be subject to the discipline of the market. For example, a considerable part of the capital stock might be owned collectively, yet production methods, composition, and scale might be regulated by competitive markets in an open, internationally oriented market economy. International competition and world prices might then provide the same sort of discipline and incentives that would obtain with a smaller government sector and a larger private sector. Sweden's economy in the 1960s provides a striking example of this possibility. As (and if) the international economy becomes more open and competitive, the economies of particular countries might become more market oriented even though the size of the nonmarket sector, as it is usually measured, might remain unchanged or even increase.

Finally, whether the characteristics associated with dynamic efficiency—namely, more rapid growth, innovation, change, and flexibility—are viewed as desirable goals or as unsettling risks depends on the eyes, hearts, and minds of the beholders. Where less rapid growth is preferred to more rapid growth, whether for reasons of environmental protection or because of the social stresses and strains said to be generated by too-rapid growth, a larger nonmarket sector may be preferred to a smaller one. In this connection, it is interesting and significant that China's development plan for the period 1986–1990 deliberately opted for "restrained growth," rather than more rapid growth, as a preferred goal of national policy. In establishing targets for China's Seventh Five-Year Plan, the Central Committee noted that "it is . . . essential to set these moderate growth rates to reduce the current excessive growth rates" in the interest of "smooth, comprehensive reform."[2]

Moreover, this preference is not confined to the leadership of Communist China. A similar stance has also been articulated by parties that remain influential in the internal politics of the United Kingdom, the Netherlands, Norway, and Sweden. And in California, antigrowth initiatives were active issues in local politics during the 1980s, through ballot referenda that sought to restrain growth by calling for restrictions on commercial and residential housing density and on other public services.

Equity Considerations

From the standpoint of equity or fairness, both market and nonmarket systems have serious flaws. Market systems do not assure equity (in the sense of reasonable equality of opportunity), although it is sometimes claimed that they do. On the one hand, the market's impersonal and relatively objective process of screening people, as well as ideas, makes an important contribution to fairness, especially when compared with other imperfect institutional inventions for performing these functions. On the other hand, inequities arise because of the very different starting points and endowments that differently situated people bring to the market's impersonal filtering process, as well as the very different degrees of good or bad luck that they encounter. It helps to have wealthy parents and a happy and stable home life; to benefit from a challenging and effective education, and to attend prestigious schools; to have talented and influential friends; to benefit from healthy and balanced nutrition; and so on. The market does not assure that such endowments will be either equal or randomly distributed.

Yet nonmarket systems are also badly flawed with respect to the equity criterion. Arbitrariness, pettiness, favoritism, and delay in bureaucratic decision making are more characteristic of nonmarket than of market organizations. Consequently, the more extensive is the role of nonmarket organization—as in collectivist, centrally planned systems—the more pervasive are these characteristics. The principal reason is that the relatively subjective authority of officialdom presides over nonmarket processes, while the relatively objective authority of trade and competition governs market processes. The catch-22 syndrome of irrationality and rigidity tends to be more frequently encountered in nonmarket than in market organizations.

In sum, the deliberate efforts of the nonmarket to remedy the types and scope of inequities generated by the market are themselves often associated with inequities of different types and scope. Surely, some degree of nonmarket intervention, activity, and redistribution is necessary to relieve the inequities of both opportunity and outcome resulting from the unbridled reign of market forces. However, the degree to which such well-intentioned intervention can extend without, in the process, making the remedy as bad as, or worse than, the original ailment is both limited and arguable.

Social and Political Dimensions: Participation and Accountability

From the standpoint of still broader and fuzzier, but not therefore less important, social and political criteria as participation and accountability, government in a pluralistic democracy presumably has certain advantages over a pure market regime.

Citizens can organize and coalesce their voting strength to bring political power to bear on government. They can participate directly or indirectly in decision making and in policy-making by using this political power to influence legislative representatives and government executives.

In similar fashion, accountability of government to the public operates through the public's power to reverse unwanted or inappropriate government actions by "throwing the rascals out" at the next election, or by maintaining a sufficiently credible threat to do so, so that the "rascals" redress or mitigate their own errors.

Despite these mechanisms, both the participation and accountability processes of government typically operate imperfectly and intermittently. More often than not, those who emerge as the effective participants and accountants are specially interested groups—comprising or representing the beneficiaries or victims of programs, rather than representing the community or the public interest as a whole. Thus, participation and accountability in the nonmarket domain usually take the form of targeted efforts by those with time, money, interests, and hence motivation, to try to shape the size and direction of nonmarket programs.

As a general rule, the successive levels of government—federal, state, and local—seem to be characterized by differing degrees of participation by and accountability to the larger publics. This rule can be formulated as a plausible principle of inverse participation and accountability: The lower the level of government, the greater public participation and government accountability are likely to be.

In contrast to this nonmarket regime, ex ante participation by the public in the marketplace is mediated through the analytic techniques of market research ("What is the market for a particular new product or service likely to be, and how soon will it materialize?"). Ex post accountability in the market context depends on dollars and cents, costs and revenues, rather than on votes or political action. The public participates in market decisions by allocating its dollars and purchasing power, rather than its voice and its vote. To survive in the market, business is accountable for covering costs with revenues—which in turn depend on the responses of the buying public.

The Role of Government in Improving and Extending Markets

As previously noted, the choice between markets and governments is not a pure or binary choice, but a matter of degree. While this matter of degree really does matter, posing the choice too sharply obscures another important issue—namely, that of uncovering opportunities by which both governments and markets can provide some improvement in the operations of the other.

A number of examples can be cited to illustrate ways in which government can contribute to improvements in the functioning of markets.

• The administrative apparatus of government includes dozens of quasi-independent agencies with extensive powers to regulate the unfettered operations of markets. Originally and ostensibly, the rule-making authority of these agencies—for example, the Federal Trade Commission, the Securities and Exchange Commission, the Interstate Commerce Commission, the Federal Communications Commission, and dozens of others—was created to avoid or reduce the failures of specific markets to produce efficient or equitable outcomes. It is timely to reconsider whether the rules established by these agencies may, in some instances and under changed conditions, currently impede rather than promote improved market operations.

For example, under the Investment Company Act of 1940 as amended, the Securities and Exchange Commission (SEC) establishes numerous and complex rules governing the multi-hundred-billion-dollar mutual funds industry. These rules cover load charges, commissions on assets, and advisers' fees that are permissible in the issuance, marketing, and management of mutual funds. The result is a maze of complex, as well as variable, regulations whose interpretation, application, and occasional circumvention consume large amounts of high-priced time of lawyers, accountants, and managers specialized in the field. The result is inflated transaction costs, as well as more rigid and less efficient markets in this field.

It would be timely to simplify this and other similar regulatory mazes that have evolved over the years. The case for zero-based budgeting has a parallel in the regulatory field, as well.

In the case of the mutual funds industry, the SEC could contribute to the operation of more efficient markets by allowing wide flexibility in the choice of local charges, fees, and asset charges, together with a strict requirement for full and transparent disclosure to prospective fund purchasers. The maze could thereby be drastically simplified, consumers would be able to make more informed choices, and mutual funds markets would function more efficiently and with lower transaction costs.

• The process by which wages are generally determined in the United States and other industrialized economies is fraught with market imperfections. Wages are often set through bargaining between quasi-monopsonistic labor unions and imperfectly competitive employers. The wage standard, including health costs and other parts of the fringe benefit package, is typically not set in relation to changes in productivity or profitability but rather in relation to sen-iority and cost of living increases, largely independent of economic performance. The well-known "stickiness" or relative inflexibility of wages that results from this process leads to larger and more unstable patterns of employment and output than would result if labor markets functioned more perfectly, and wages were more closely linked with productivity and profitability.

To improve the functioning of labor markets, Martin Weitzman has proposed that wages be determined as a negotiated *share* of employer revenues, rather than as a fixed standard established independently of performance. Thus, when revenues rose, the specified share would result in higher realized wages; when revenues fell, the wage repre-sented by the specified share would decline accordingly. While the share would be fixed in advance, realized wages would be tied to actual output and revenues, and hence employment and production would tend to be sustained at higher levels. Employers would have a greater incentive to increase employment in prosperous years and less of an incentive to reduce employment in slack ones. Both labor and plant capacity would thus be utilized more fully and more efficiently.[3] If such a "share-wage" system would in fact enable labor markets to function more efficiently than the standard wage determination process, it may be appro-priate for government to provide various types of induce-ments to encourage the development of such a system—for example, by publicizing and documenting various modes of instituting share-wage practices;[4] by some adjustment in the tax rate applied to share-wage income in cases where the effect of sharing is to reduce an individual's wage in-come substantially from what it had previously been; and by treating some of the possible added costs on employers from experimentation with a new share-wage system as expensable research and development costs.

• The market for health care is especially rife with imperfections that impose high costs and large inefficiencies on the economy. Paradoxically, some of these imperfections have actually resulted from intensified efforts to make the provision of health care itself more subject to competitive market pressures. For example, the growth of competitive sources for laboratory and other ancillary services has led an increasing number of practicing physicians to acquire financial interests in firms providing the supporting medical services that these physicians themselves often recommend to their patients: diagnostic laboratories, radiologic imaging centers, ambulatory clinics and surgery centers, physical therapy centers, dialysis units, and other such facilities. That conflicts of interest may arise in such instances—when physicians act as both demanders and suppliers—is evident and significant. Higher health costs and overuse of the facilities may be encouraged because the physicians themselves derive lucrative, if indirect, returns in the process. One approach to remedying this type of market failure—identified by its critics as "the threat of entrepreneurialism" in the medical profession—is to exhort doctors themselves to adhere to their professional ethics as a means of reversing these practices.[5] For those of us who are skeptical of the effectiveness of such exhortation, some governmental intervention may also have an important role to play. For example, California law currently requires that physicians must disclose any financial interest they have in free-standing diagnostic facilities to which they refer their patients. Legislation to prohibit such referrals regardless of disclosure has been discussed in the state legislature but not enacted.

Clearly, in such instances, one is risking the possibility of nonmarket failure—for example, the incentives toward bureaucratic empire building through internalities and redundant costs—to avoid the existing market failure of negative externalities and imperfections in the medical marketplace.

• Another example of how government action may be able to help improve and extend the functioning of markets arises in connection with corporate pension funds. In this instance, improved functioning of the financial markets would result from both revising and reducing the existing regulation embodied in the Employee Retirement Income Security Act (ERISA). This legislation was enacted for the ostensible purpose of protecting retirement funds so that their intended beneficiaries would receive their proper retirement benefits.

Pension funds constitute enormous holdings of wealth and represent a major continuing source of capital formation in the United States and other industrialized countries. In 1989 the total assets in private U.S. pension funds amounted to almost 2 trillion dollars, representing 6 percent of the nation's total financial assets.[6] To regulate the accumulation and use of these funds, ERISA has mandated certain rules relating to funding obligations by employers and also providing for the establishment of the Pension Benefit Guarantee Corporation (PBGC) to provide insurance that retirement benefits will be protected. Although ERISA provides an extensive structure of regulations with attendant administrative operating costs, the system's structure allows for, and indeed almost assures, serious underfunding of pension funds in the aggregate.

For example, the latitude provided for varying actuarial assumptions in corporate calculations of benefit obligations permits companies to make the unrealistic assumption that workers will not receive further wage increases, thereby adding to pension obligations. This assumption therefore results in underestimation of the obligations of most retirement funds to finance the pensions of employees in the period when they approach retirement.

Furthermore, because pension benefits are insured by PBGC, companies are themselves only nominally responsible for such underfunded obligations. The additional risks of underfunding are transferred to PBGC, which itself has only limited financial claims on companies that subsequently terminate their underfunded pension plans or simply turn out to be unable to meet their contingent pension obligations.[7]

To make the situation even murkier, the insurance premiums charged by PBGC are both too low and unrelated to pension risks, which vary quite widely across the range of companies covered by the system. Since PBGC started in 1974, it has accumulated substantial operating deficits because its premium income has been inadequate to cover losses from termination of underfunded pension plans.

Man Bing Sze has confirmed empirically that the private pension system as a whole is substantially underfunded, and that "the problem is much more severe than is commonly perceived."[8] One approach to alleviating this situation would be to impose more severe and extensive regulatory restrictions on the operation of pension funds—for example, changing the actuarial assumptions that companies in the system would be obliged to follow; or establishing insurance premiums for coverage by PBGC that would be substantially higher than at the present time, and also would differentiate markedly according to the degree of risk associated with the prevailing pension fund obligations and financial circumstances of each of the companies covered by the system.

Obviously, going this route would entail still larger bureaucratic costs by both government and the private sector to apply these more exacting rules.

There is, however, another route for reducing and revising existing regulation of pension funds that would enable the financial marketplace to function more efficiently and at the same time reduce the regulatory costs of assuring a sound

and sensible pension system. The policy innovation proposed by Sze is to give pensions a first claim on corporate
assets, thereby using the discipline of the financial markets
themselves to assure that pension promises are kept. In
other words, when a company is obliged to assume full
pension liabilities, all of the company's assets would be
behind the obligations incurred by the pension funds. The
financial market could then be relied upon to evaluate the
risk to which different companies were exposed by the
reserves they have accumulated in relation to their pension
fund obligations, and the market would allocate the costs
of this commitment of corporate assets. Stated differently,
the market value of common stocks would adjust to the
corporation's income and wealth prospects *net* of its pension
obligations.[9]

For a major change of this sort to take place, Congress
would have to pass amended legislation. Once this was
done, many of the ERISA regulations could be substantially
streamlined, and financial markets could function effectively in policing the pension system.

• The essential point common to all the foregoing examples
can be illustrated with one final example in the field of
antitrust legislation. The legislative and administrative antitrust structure in the United States is designed to reduce,
if not entirely preclude, the occurrence of market failure in
the form of monopolistic practices arising from increasing
returns to scale, or from other sources. Thus, the Sherman
Antitrust Act of 1890 makes it illegal to fix prices in restraint
of trade, and the Clayton Act of 1914 prohibits mergers and
acquisitions that "may reduce competition" or "may tend
to create a monopoly."

The aim of these antitrust provisions is to avoid undue
concentration in any industry on the grounds that, even if
some short-run efficiency gains might ensue from such con-

centration, efficiency would be jeopardized in the long run because competition would be stifled. Hence, it is argued that the full realization of potential economies of scale in the short run should be disallowed, lest greater inefficiency result from excessive concentration of economic power in the long run.

This effort to make markets function more efficiently may, in fact, concentrate on the wrong markets. Under current world economic conditions, and barring the emergence of severe protectionism, competition in many industries—for example, in electronics, communications, machinery, petrochemicals—arises principally from large international firms, rather than from local national ones. With the pervasive internationalization of markets that has occurred in recent years, the effectiveness of competition does not depend on "small is good, big is bad"—the shibboleth that was accepted in the past. Instead, the effectiveness of competition depends on the openness of domestic markets to imports.

Consequently, it may be timely to consider seriously, as Malcolm Baldridge has proposed, some revision of U.S. antitrust legislation to allow mergers and acquisitions to occur even if they "may tend to" create more concentration in particular national markets. The result of such revision might enable markets to function more efficiently, and prices to be lower and product quality higher, due to less restraint on the development of larger-scale organizations able to realize greater efficiency gains from larger-scale units, even if these would contravene previously existing antitrust restraints.[10]

All of the foregoing examples illustrate a common theme: Government can sometimes undertake initiatives—in legal as well as regulatory and administrative domains—to improve and extend the functioning of markets, thereby reducing the incidence of market failures.

The Role of Government in Transforming Command Systems into Market Economies

The most extreme version of the role of government in "extending and improving markets" arises in the historical process under way in the 1990s of transforming the non-market command economies of Eastern Europe, Russia, Ukraine, and the other republics of the former Soviet Union into market-based systems.

The generic problems of transformation are essentially the same whether the locale is the former Soviet Union, Eastern Europe, China, or many of the centrally controlled economies of the Third World. To be sure, there are differences in historical circumstances, cultural affinities, institutional antecedents, and the existing physical, social, and political infrastructures. But the differences, while important, are incidental to an essentially similar task. Transformation depends on implementing simultaneously, or at least contemporaneously, a package of six closely linked and mutually supporting elements, and government policy must play an essential role in all of them.

1. Monetary reform to ensure control of the money supply and credit

2. Fiscal control to assure budgetary balance and to limit monetization of a budget deficit if one occurs

3. Price and wage deregulation to link prices and wages to costs and productivity, respectively

4. Privatization, legal protection of property rights, and the breakup of state monopolies to provide for competition, as well as worker and management incentives that reflect changes in relative market prices

5. A social safety net to protect those who may become unemployed as transformation proceeds

6. Currency convertibility to link the transforming economy to the world economy and to competition in international markets

The first two elements (monetary reform and fiscal control) and the fifth (the social safety net) create the broad macroeconomic environment that enables the incentive mechanisms of the other three to move resources toward more efficient and growth-promoting uses. The government's role is both crucial and paradoxical: crucial in initiating all of the elements, yet paradoxical because the process that the government initiates is intended to diminish its ensuing role, displace its overextended functions, and reduce its size in favor of market mechanisms.

Each of the six elements is less likely to be effective without the reciprocal support provided by the others. Hence, attempts to reform nonmarket economies by piecemeal steps are more likely to founder than to succeed.

Consider, for example, the link between the first two elements. Monetary reform is necessary to limit growth of the money supply to a rate that accords with the growth of real output. It is also a necessary means of providing access to credit on the basis of borrowers' economic capabilities and their associated risks, rather than on the basis of their political connections or credentials. A competent entrepreneur with a good idea should be able to obtain credit not available to someone whose principal distinction is membership in the governing political party or kinship to a government official.

Fiscal reform requires a budget process that constrains government expenditures to a level close to revenues and precludes or limits "off-budget" subsidies and other transactions that would disrupt monetary discipline, as well as budgetary balance. Recourse to extra-budgetary subsidies to bail out deficit-ridden state enterprises has been a standard procedure in the Soviet Union, China, and other command economies. Fiscal and monetary reform should preclude its recurrence. Usually, the complementarity between monetary reform and fiscal reform is facilitated by institutional separation between the finance ministry (or treasury), and the central bank or banking system.

In turn, the third element—deregulation of prices and wages—requires monetary and fiscal restraint if prices and wages are to be linked to real costs and productivity, while avoiding general inflation. Goods that are in short supply or are costly to produce should experience price increases relative to those that are more abundant and less costly. In turn, these price increases provide signals and incentives for increased and more efficient production. Similarly, wages paid for more productive labor and skills should be expected to rise relative to those that are less productive. The newly established parities among costs and prices should operate in the public sector as well as the private sector.

For deregulation of prices and wages to promote efficient use of resources, the fourth element—privatization, legal protection of property rights, and the breakup of state monopolies into competing entities—must be implemented at the same time. This requires an appropriate legal code and appropriate procedures for resolving disputes over property transactions and acquisitions, as well as litigation associated with prior ownership claims. It also requires a choice among several ways of changing from state ownership to private ownership—an issue about which there is considerable controversy among policymakers, economists, lawyers, and financiers.

For example, equity shares in state enterprises can be issued to workers and management, while reserving some of the shares for local government and foreign investors (resale of the shares with or without a specified holding period can also be invoked). This method has the advantage of simplicity and clarity; its putative disadvantage is the ostensible unfairness of a process in which some of the new shareholders would be losers while others would realize gains, due in both cases to the arbitrary circumstance of where they had been previously employed.

Another mode of privatization is to issue enterprise shares to the general public on a random basis rather than determining enterprise ownership on the basis of employment. In this case, everyone has an equal chance of picking a winner or loser among the hundreds or thousands of state enterprises that typically exist in command economies. Windfall gains that result from a random process are, it can be argued, more equitable than those that result from the accident of prior employment.

Perhaps the simplest method of privatization is to auction enterprises to the highest bidder—limiting or excluding participation by nonnationals. This method, favored by Czech economist (and Prime Minister) Vaclav Klaus and others, has sometimes been criticized on the grounds that those most likely to have ample funds to win the bidding are black marketeers and former Communist Party nomenklatura.

Still another method is to issue public vouchers representing potential claims on the shares of enterprises to be privatized. Foreign bankers or mutual fund managers would be invited to bid for the public vouchers. The public would then trade their vouchers for shares in the mutual funds that appealed to them.

All of these methods would result in the creation of a resale market for equities and mutual fund shares. Contrary to some of the debate on this issue, none of the methods requires that state enterprises be carefully evaluated before privatization is accomplished. Choosing among the alternative methods does require assessment of their respective advantages (for example, simplicity, comprehensibility, and speed), as well as their disadvantages (for example, distributional unfairness and inequity).

In any event, whichever method or methods of privatization are selected—and experimentation with several is advisable because none is clearly preferable to the others—their success remains linked to the other elements of the transformation package. Unless rewards are linked to asset ownership, and unless such rewards can be accumulated legally, incentives to innovate and to increase productivity will be impaired. Effective supply responses to price and wage deregulation depend on the incentives provided by private ownership and accumulation. Moreover, private ownership is essential for market forces to provide an effective stick, as well as carrot. If ownership is in the hands of the state, the discipline imposed by market competition will be attenuated, if not eliminated. When state enterprises are confronted by losses, they typically evade or ignore the threat of bankruptcy that private enterprises would face if confronted by similar losses.

In moving from command to market economies, private ownership plays a crucial role by providing the incentive structure required for markets to function efficiently. Avoiding socially unacceptable disparities in income distribution is a responsibility of public expenditure and tax policies, within the context of private ownership and market competition.

The fifth element—establishment of a social security system as a safety net—is also essential for the transformation process to succeed. Without it, the process may create fear of widespread unemployment, social stress, and political instability, thereby seriously impeding the transition.

In most command economies, social protection—against illness, disability, age, and unemployment—has principally been the responsibility of state enterprises. As privatization proceeds, these responsibilities are likely to become one of the principal functions of government, financed by taxation and by payments levied on the insured. In the initial stage of transformation, taxation will probably have to bear most of the burden, although the real incremental burden imposed on the economy by the social safety net is likely to be less than is usually assumed.

The final element—currency convertibility—is essential to complete the transformation process by linking internal markets and their prices, wages, productivities, and technologies to those of international markets. This linkage provides the opportunity for comparative costs and comparative advantage to operate for the benefit of the transforming national economy. With a convertible currency, the transforming economy can determine those goods and services it can produce at relatively low cost compared to the costs of other countries and those it produces at relatively high cost. In response to convertibility, exports of the relatively low-cost goods will expand, as will imports of the relatively high-cost ones.

If the other elements of the package—especially monetary and fiscal discipline and market-determined prices—are effectively implemented, currency convertibility with a floating exchange rate can be embarked upon and sustained with minimal hard currency reserves, contrary to a frequent argument about the need for large reserves as a precondition for convertibility.

The interactions and mutually supporting relationships among the six elements of the transformation process are summarized in figure 8.1. The lines indicate the contribution by one element to the effectiveness of another element to which the arrowhead points. (For example, monetary and fiscal reform contribute to the effectiveness of price and wage deregulation.)

In sum, the process of transforming command, nonmarket economies to market ones is both better understood and

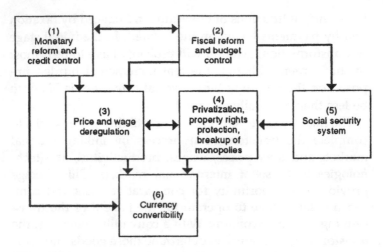

Figure 8.1
Components of transformation of command economies.

more tractable than might be inferred from much of the public debate. Transformation is a systems process encompassing the interactive and mutually supporting elements described previously. And the role of government and public policy is of central importance in the entire process. Ironically, the principal responsibility for creating and extending the market's role while redefining and delimiting that of government rests with the government itself.[11]

The Potential Role of Market Forces in Improving the Functioning of Government

Just as new government policies, and changes in old ones, may contribute to improving the functioning of markets, so may market processes and incentives contribute to improving the functioning of government—the nonmarket. In other words, the incidence of nonmarket failure might be diminished by injecting some elements of market forces into government operations.

One area in which many of the characteristic nonmarket failures arise in government is defense procurement. Expenditures for procurement of weapons systems and military equipment currently amounts to about $65 billion in 1992, including development and procurement costs for the Army, Navy, and Air Force.[12] These procurements are often afflicted by cost escalation and schedule slippages, and sometimes by imperfect technical performance of the finally procured systems. The sources of nonmarket failure that characterize the process are abundant—for example, incentives in the individual services and commands to maximize budgets rather than to minimize costs; a recurring pattern of rising and redundant costs over the lifetimes of development and procurement of particular systems; and inequitable, politically based awards of contracts through tacit or direct logrolling between the services and the cognizant congressional committees.

Frequently, the defense procurement process for major weapons systems procurement is also characterized by the creation of a de facto monopoly by a single producer who acquires prime responsibility for producing a particular weapons system after the initial bidding and testing stages have been concluded. If a single producer acquires responsibility for a particular aircraft or tank or missile system, the resulting monopolistic position tends to reduce pressure toward efficiency; cost overruns and schedule slippages may thereby ensue. To ease the problem, one might try to inject competitive discipline into a market that involves only a single procurement source.

Various remedies, if not solutions, may be considered. For example, even after a single-source procurement contract has been let, it may be possible to preserve the downstream contestability of the market through various means: assuring that information about plant tooling and specifications is available to potential future entrants; allowing for the possibility of leasing by subsequent bidders of the production lines built by the initial prime contractor; including as part of the initial bid and contract procedure a requirement for warranties on the cost and performance of the end product.[13]

Another example of the opportunity to inject some of the discipline and incentives of market forces into nonmarket activities in a very different field is the possible use of educational vouchers *within* the public school system. It can be granted that education, especially at primary and secondary levels, is a quasi-public good, because society realizes distinct benefits from improved education beyond the private, individual benefits that would be reflected in market pricing of education. Nevertheless, it is still worth considering how competition, experimentation, innovation, and flexibility can be enhanced in the public school system. A possible solution is for public schools located in the same or contiguous school districts to compete for individual student vouchers that would carry with them financial stipends. Hence, the budgets of particular schools would be subject to increases or decreases to the extent that they attracted or lost students and their accompanying stipends, in response to the quality and attraction of their curricula.[14]

For example, if a particular primary school or high school had especially strong offerings in English, or in science, or in basic mathematics, and if these special attributes resulted in a higher demand for enrollment in that school, its budget would rise by the addition of the vouchers tendered by the students enrolling in it. The result would be that schools and school systems would have incentives to experiment, to innovate, and to compete, while still operating within the public school framework as a whole. Thus, some degree of consumer sovereignty would be injected into an institution and a process that normally is characterized by very substantial inertia. Parents would be the ostensible arbiters of this process, retaining the burden of responsibility to shift their children among at least a subset of competing schools. By thereby providing a dose of consumer sovereignty, the same type of incentives and discipline would be injected into the educational nonmarket in the public sector that typically characterize the market in the private sector. The counterargument, that consumers—that is, parents—are not sufficiently well-informed to exercise this responsibility, has some validity in the short run but less merit in the longer run. At the least, extensive experimentation with a voucher system would seem worthwhile.

Charles Schultze has emphasized this general approach as a means of improving the functioning of government in a book aptly titled *The Public Use of Private Interest*.[15] The essence of the approach is to redress, if not reverse, the usual presumption that social and economic reform implies public sector intervention to improve the admitted shortcomings of the market. Instead, effective reforms may sometimes lie in extending market processes into the workings of the nonmarket, or government, sector.

As Schultze points out, "We think of the public sector as intervening in the private sector, and not vice versa."[16] Several potential advantages can be realized by reversing this bias, and having marketlike processes and incentives intrude on the functioning of the nonmarket sector, rather than having government intrude on the functioning of the market. One potential advantage is to reduce the need for coercive intervention and bureaucratized intrusions by government into society at large. Another potential benefit lies in reducing the government's need for information as well as detailed, and frequently flawed, cost-benefit analyses to guide its regulatory intervention. Finally, a market approach to governmental reform can provide incentives for technological change in the private sector in socially desirable directions in such areas as pollution control, reduced traffic congestion, and improved environmental quality.[17]

While indirect and roundabout ways of accomplishing social objectives may thus have much to recommend them, they usually receive less public attention than do legislation or administrative regulations. Schultze suggests the reason is that legislators and government officials do not understand how markets, competition, and prices actually work to promote efficient change.[18] One might add to this explanation the not infrequent self-interest of legislators and bureaucrats in having nonmarket activity take the form of direct, organized intervention, rather than indirect, roundabout incentives, because larger staffs, budgets, and personal, political, and professional advancement often lie in the latter directions.

Schultze offers a number of examples for applying this approach to the conduct of government—for example, supporting higher education by allowing students to "buy" education where they choose, rather than directly subsidizing colleges and universities; issuing vouchers to individuals to enable them to choose particular manpower-training and skill-enhancing programs, rather than providing direct grants for these purposes to educational and training institutions; applying a tax on emission of chemical or noise pollutants, rather than specifying precise levels of permissible emissions. In each case, a quasi-market process is introduced that is likely to promote adaptation and innovation in the nonmarket sector along lines that are more efficient as well as socially desirable.

Anthony Pascal has shown, in a RAND study, how market forces can be introduced into the operations of local government through the application of beneficiary charges as a partial substitute for taxes in the financing of some public services.[19]

Another extension of this approach may lie in the creation of a "privatization ombudsman" as an independent agency in government, with the responsibility to look for governmental functions that might gradually and usefully be privatized.[20] The ombudsman function would be analogous to what the Agency for International Development has been trying to introduce in its foreign aid activities through "privatization feasibility studies." The aim of such a privatization ombudsman function would not be to provide detailed market research for prospective venture capitalists, but to do sufficient analysis of the relevant costs and benefits associated with privatizing some activities of the nonmarket sector so that better decisions could be made.[21]

It is worth noting that the issue of privatization can be viewed from two different, and unrelated, perspectives: one perspective concerns the relative efficiency of private versus public ownership and utilization of assets presently owned by the government; the other concerns the contribution that sales of government assets can make toward reducing the level of reported federal budget deficits. The efficiency perspective is the one that is emphasized in the preceding discussion. The deficit-reducing perspective is not only different but largely illusory—it simply involves a short-run change in the government's balance sheet (if one were maintained), with little, if any, effect on credit markets because the ensuing reduction in governmental borrowing would simply be offset by an equivalent increase in private borrowing to finance private purchases of government assets.

The idea of a privatization ombudsman as an agency and a function *within* government may appear on the face of it as a contradiction in terms. Nevertheless, it is not inconceivable that such an evaluation and reorganization function could be built into the operations of government if the incentive approach discussed in connection with "the public use of private interest" were combined with a reasonable degree of organizational ingenuity. Moreover, the opportunity to introduce this approach may be enhanced by separating "production" of an initially public sector activity from the "funding" function; the production effort could perhaps be gradually privatized, while funding responsibilities were initially maintained through tax financing. Recent experimentation with private contracting for the construction and operation of prisons, financed by tightly constrained public sector budgets, provides an example of this approach.[22]

Market and Nonmarket Systems: Dilemmas and Pitfalls

As previously noted, the choice between markets and governments is not a pure choice but a matter of degree. Yet the degree that is chosen matters a great deal from the standpoint of both the economic and the social performance of the resulting system: the more the systemic choice favors the market, the more the system confronts the pitfalls and shortcomings of market failure; and the more the systemic choice favors the nonmarket, the more the resulting system confronts the pitfalls and shortcomings of nonmarket failure. From the standpoint of effective economic performance, the record strongly suggests that the shortcomings of nonmarket failure overwhelm those associated with market failure. Market systems simply and decisively perform better than nonmarket systems in static as well as dynamic terms, and in terms of both short-run allocative efficiency and long-term economic growth.

Advocates of nonmarket systems, however, rebut this conclusion by arguing that other dimensions of system performance—for example, social equity, public participation, and accountability—are at least as important in evaluating system performance as the efficiency and growth dimensions. According to these criteria, the contention is that nonmarket systems compete with market systems on much more favorable terms, in both an absolute and a relative sense.

I do not here attempt to resolve this issue. However, it seems evident that, at least for the most extreme versions of the nonmarket system choice, performance according to these noneconomic criteria varies from poor to dismal. The basis of this judgment is the record of the most extreme versions of the nonmarket systemic choice—namely, the former Soviet Union during the decades preceding its dissolution in 1992 and North Korea, two national systems most tightly and pervasively controlled by nonmarket organizations and processes. For example, with respect to social equity, these systems enunciated a declaratory policy of a classless society, while, in fact, the difference in living standards, privileges, and power of the ruling *nomenklatura* compared with those of the masses of the former Soviet and North Korean publics probably exceeds the gap between the Forbes 400 and the average worker in the United States. With respect to standards of social equity and progress, statistics covering health, housing, and longevity displayed a surprising deterioration in conditions for the masses of Soviet society, while the *nomenklatura* received some of the best medical and health care available anywhere in the world.[23]

A comparable evaluation of the relative performance of North and South Korea is more difficult because the corresponding evidence is less accessible. Nevertheless, in general, the comparison between the predominantly market-oriented South Korean system and the highly centralized nonmarket North Korean system exhibits features similar to those cited in informed comparisons between the United States and the Soviet Union prior to its dissolution. Economic growth and development in the South vastly exceeds that in the North. Moreover, the circumstances with respect to power, privilege, and living conditions of the ruling political and military class in the North probably separate it even more sharply from the masses of the North Korean populace than the distributional spread that is found in the South.[24]

These observations do not imply that the path and prospects of market systems are easy and bright. Their problems, while surely different, are formidable.

The dilemmas and pitfalls of market and nonmarket systems are fundamentally grounded in their political contexts and institutions: in the institutions of pluralist and capitalist democracy in the case of the U.S. political economy, and in the institutions of the central command oligarchy that characterized the Soviet Union before its breakup, and still hold sway in China.

The effective functioning of market systems can be seriously eroded by pluralistic, democratic processes. The erosion arises because of the incentives that these processes create for steadily increasing encroachment by nonmarket forces on the effective functioning of the market. These incentives result from the separation or decoupling between those who receive the benefits and those who pay the costs of government programs. The classic free rider problem is a special case of such decoupling; benefits are received regardless of whether any particular individual pays, and consequently the incentive for individuals to pay voluntarily is attenuated.

We have previously discussed the two separate aspects of this decoupling phenomenon: microdecoupling and macrodecoupling. Macrodecoupling creates a political opportunity and an economic incentive to expand redistributive programs. Whereas microdecoupling implies that a well-organized minority may exploit the majority, macrodecoupling implies that the majority may exploit the minority. In the absence of self-restraint by the majority, macrodecoupling can erode the mainsprings of investment, innovation, and growth, if the majority's incentive to redistribute weakens the minority's incentive to invest, to innovate, and to expand. This is not to deny the contrary proposition: that limiting the minority's affluence may be essential to assure that sufficient social harmony is maintained in a market-oriented political-economic system.[25]

As noted earlier, the enormous expansion of entitlement and other social programs in the United States and in Western Europe since the mid-1960s is a reflection of this decoupling phenomenon. Because of this expansion, perhaps half of the U.S. population depend, at least in part, on federal aid in one form or another![26] The comparable figures for Western Europe would show even more dramatic growth of dependence by a large proportion of the population on income transfers from the more affluent minority.

The result of such trends may be to erode the effective functioning of market systems. Economic growth rates in Western Europe generally fell between the early 1970s and the early 1980s, before rebounding slightly in the late 1980s, during a time when public sector expenditures rose from less than 40 percent of the European Economic Community's GNP to nearly 50 percent in the early 1980s, before leveling off to roughly 48 percent in 1989. At the same time, though productivity has lagged, real wages in Western Europe rose one-third faster than in the United States. And this rise in real wages contributed to the sharp rise in European unemployment and consequent slower economic growth. While employment in Western Europe remained virtually unchanged between 1975 and 1990, unemployment rose from 4 or 5 percent to 10 percent during this period. By contrast, in the United States, employment increased by more than 18 million jobs.[27]

Thus, the pluralistic and capitalistic market systems of Western democracies face profound dilemmas and distortions. The principal culprits include, first, the often high time-discounts of elected officials, resulting from the pressure of relatively short intervals between election campaigns and, second, the decoupling between those who benefit from and those who pay for nonmarket programs, frequently resulting in stronger incentives to expand than to limit government programs. As a result, such programs may be initiated or expanded even though they are inefficient in a microeconomic sense (for example, tariffs, agricultural price supports, import quotas, and other restrictions), as well as inequitable in conferring special gains and privileges on politically effective groups, while imposing greater costs on politically less effective ones. Other programs may be expanded to a level where they become inefficient in a dynamic sense (e.g., entitlement programs) by undermining the incentives on which the economy's longer-term growth depend.

Nevertheless, there remains a potential, although imperfect and unreliable, opportunity for resolution or at least mitigation of these shortcomings through the democratic process. This process allows the opponents and victims, who are often the voters and taxpayers at large, to mobilize their dispersed interests to reverse the policies and programs that may have erred by overexpansion or misdirection. The political marketplace thus provides the possibility of reversing the myopia and distortions of the political process itself. Something of this sort was certainly at work in the reversal of policy direction implied by the election of Ronald Reagan in November 1980 and again in November 1984 in the United States, as well as in the mandate received by the Conservative party in the United Kingdom in 1979, and again, if more narrowly, in 1992. The same process, at the state rather than national level, has resulted in the passage of citizen-initiated legislation in California, Massachusetts, and other states rolling back the level of property taxes and placing a cap on subsequent increases.

The dilemmas and pitfalls of nonmarket systems, associated with their centrally commanded oligarchies, are even more formidable than those that jeopardize market systems. These dilemmas arise from the fundamental dialectical contradictions that are peculiar to and inherent in nonmarket systems. In these systems, a dilemma arises from the conflict between the political demands for centralized control and the economic demands for decentralization, competition, experimentation, and innovation that derive directly from the increasing complexity, diversity, and multiplicity of opportunities in modern economies. Modern technology places a premium on acquiring, analyzing, and interpreting the wealth of available information concerning alternative production methods, new products and services, alternative distribution systems, alternative opportunities for using and for saving resources, and the innumerable, if not infinite, opportunities available under these technological conditions for trial and error. Markets, and the prices they generate, provide abundant and constantly updated sources of economic information that centrally controlled nonmarket systems eschew and suppress.

There is a logical, as well as empirical, reason that decentralized market decision making meets the challenges and opportunities posed by new technology more effectively than does centralized nonmarket decision making. The political economy of command oligarchic systems concentrates and centralizes decision making in the familiar institutional triad characterizing these systems—namely, the controlling single party, the state security apparatus, and the military. In practice, as well as theory, the formal "government" acts as the administrative agent of these elite institutions that are at the helm of centralized political power. The tension that results is fundamental: on the one side is the concentration and centralization of power required for assuring political control, and on the other side is the dispersal of decision making that is necessary for economic efficiency and technological progress.

The result of this tension has been evident in the performance of most of the nonmarket, centrally planned economies in recent decades. These economies have been beset by declining rates of growth, rising capital-output ratios, declining factor productivity, and falling or near-stagnant health, longevity, and consumption standards. China has been a rare exception to this pattern of performance in nonmarket systems. Its experiments with "market socialism" and decentralized decision making, using market prices as at least a partial guide for a widening range of allocative decisions, have been at least moderately successful. It remains to be seen whether a durable, as well as effective, combination of legitimacy with control can be obtained and maintained by the Communist party if significant elements of a market system are grafted onto what is fundamentally and ideologically a quintessentially nonmarket system.

Moreover, there is a sense in which the term market socialism is an oxymoron. On the one hand, socialism rests fundamentally on the premise of collective ownership, as well as collective utilization, of the means of production, while the market rests fundamentally on the premise that ownership and utilization are governed by competition, prices, property rights, and accumulation.

In sum, centrally planned, nonmarket oligarchies confront dialectical inconsistencies and contradictions in political, ideological, technological, and economic terms, which accounts for their demise in Eastern Europe and the Soviet Union, their uncertain longevity in China and North Korea, and their diminished support in the Third World. Such systems foreclose—by virtue of their extreme concentration of political power—the potential remedy available to capitalist and pluralist democracies through a more open and competitive political process. This process provides both a potential remedy and a social solvent. In its absence, the central planning authorities in nonmarket systems tend to be captured by their own commitments and pronouncements, and midcourse corrections tend to be foreclosed. Such systems are therefore prone to stagnation and deterioration, on the one hand, or to explosive social change, on the other, because their structure inhibits debate, experimentation, and gradual reform. The historic events of the late 1980s and early 1990s in Eastern Europe and the former Soviet Union provide striking illustrations of the fault lines in these systems.

Notes

1. Viner (1960).

2. Xinhua (1985).

3. See Weitzman (1984).

4. Ibid., 142–145.

5. See the *New England Journal of Medicine* (1985, 749–751).

6. See Sze (1985, 1ff), and Federal Reserve System (1990).

7. Ibid.

8. Ibid., 6ff.

9. Ibid., 7ff.

10. See Baldridge (1985).

11. For a more complete exposition, see Wolf (1991).

12. Department of Commerce (1991).

13. See Baumol, Panzar, and Willig (1982); Palfry and Romer (1983); and Rogerson (1992).

14. For a recent exposition of this device, see Chubb and Moe (1986). The voucher proposal also has received support from the 1986 report of the Carnegie Forum on Education and the Economy.

15. Schultze (1977).

16. Ibid., 13.

17. Ibid., 19–25.

18. Ibid., 78.

19. Pascal et al. (1984).

20. This idea was suggested by Timothy Wolf in a memorandum to the author, and it is also implicit in Savas (1982).

21. The Office of Management and Budget sometimes performs part of this role in connection with preparation of the federal budget. The function is also implicit in the idea of periodic zero-based budgeting for government activities outside of government. Mexico's Office for Privatization of State-Owned Enterprise performs this function, as well as implementing its results. See Rogozinski (1992). For an account of privatization and related efforts at state and local levels in the United States, see Osborne and Gaebler (1992).

22. This type of separation between "production" and "funding" arises in the framework developed by Randy Ross (1988) for analyzing the roles and missions of government and the private sector.

23. See Voslensky (1984, 178–241), Feshbach (1982), Feshbach and Davis (1980), and Bernstam (1987).

24. See Wolf et al. (1985).

25. See Viner (1960). As Viner points out (p. 68), "No modern people will have zeal for the free market unless it operates in a setting of 'distributive justice' with which they are tolerably content."

26. See Feldstein (1980).

27. See Wolf (1985), and OECD (1992).

Appendix A
Nonmarket Demand, Supply, and Equilibria

The Nonmarket Demand Function

In light of the characteristics of nonmarket demand described in chapter 3, we can specify, as a heuristic device, a function indicating the aggregate demand for nonmarket activities, and the component demands for particular nonmarket activities, as follows:

$$D_i(\hat{X}, \hat{M}, \hat{I}, \hat{G}, \hat{E}, R, P, Y) \tag{1}$$

and

$$D = \sum_1^n D_i \tag{2}$$

where

D_i = demand for the ith nonmarket output, with $i = 1, 2, \ldots n$ (for government activities, the n outputs fall within the four general types described in the text)

D = aggregate demand for the n nonmarket activities (expressed in dollars, because of the difficulty of measuring many nonmarket outputs in physical units, and the accounting convention of expressing nonmarket outputs as equal to their input costs)

$\hat{X} =$ perceived externalities resulting from market activities (expressed in dollars—see equation (3) in note 1)[1]

$\hat{M} =$ perceived degree of monopoly (perhaps measured by the concentration of industry, or by the difference between prevailing prices of market goods and their competitive prices)

$\hat{I} =$ perceived market imperfections (including barriers to entry, discriminatory access to credit, the extent of patent or other technological restrictions, etc., perhaps measured as a qualitatively scaled variable)

$\hat{G} =$ perceived need or demand for pure public goods such as defense (measured in dollar terms, by the (vertical) summation of individual demands for public goods)

$\hat{E} =$ perceived inequities, reflecting some specified standard of equity (e.g., according to equality of outcome, or equality of opportunity; or equity according to Rawls, or Marx, or the Old Testament, or the New Testament), and measured accordingly (e.g., by an appropriate Gini coefficient, or a qualitatively scaled variable)[2]

$R =$ the tax rate

$P =$ the cost of a "unit" of nonmarket activity (because of the aforementioned difficulty of measuring nonmarket output in physical units, this cost may be measured as the average input cost per worker-year of nonmarket activity, e.g., the average government wage),

$Y =$ national income (expressed in dollars)

The circumflex over a variable denotes the *perceived*, rather than the actual, level of the variable, as discussed later and in chapter 3.

In accord with the previous discussion of characteristics of demand, the partial derivatives of aggregate nonmarket demand D, with respect to $\hat{M}$, $\hat{I}$, $\hat{G}$, $\hat{E}$, and the absolute value of $\hat{X}$, are expected to be positive, although the partial derivatives of some of the separate D_i's with respect to each of these variables may be zero. For example, the demand for defense-related nonmarket output will presumably be unaffected by the perceived degree of monopoly, or externalities, or social inequities. On the other hand, the demand for regulatory programs will be affected by the perceived degree of monopoly and of externalities, and the demand for income transfers will be affected by perceived inequities.

The partial derivatives of aggregate nonmarket demand D, with respect to the tax rate R and the wage cost P, are presumed to be negative.[3] In a rough sense, R is the "tax price" associated with nonmarket activity, so both the D_i's and aggregate D will tend to fall as R rises. The government wage rate P is a particular factor cost of nonmarket output to which taxpayers (voters) may be especially sensitive. If government wage rates rise (relative to nongovernment wages), public reaction may be invidious and adverse, and public demand for nonmarket activity can be expected to diminish.

National income, Y, is included in the demand function on the premise that there is likely to be a positive income elasticity of demand for nonmarket output, as there is for most market output. However, this premise is perhaps more arguable in the case of nonmarket than market demand. For some of the n nonmarket activities (for example, those relating to the administration of social welfare and other redistributive programs), demand may vary *inversely* with Y: the demand for certain nonmarket activities may be higher in business cycle troughs than at the peaks.

But even if, on balance, *aggregate* nonmarket demand tends toward a positive income elasticity, there is yet another complication. If the tax structure is progressive, the effect on nonmarket demand of a change in real income, Y, may be offset by the interaction between the income change and the resulting changes in the average tax rate and aggregate tax take. While higher income will incline voters toward increased nonmarket demand, the higher percentage tax liability resulting from their higher income will tend to diminish nonmarket demand.[4]

The Nonmarket Supply Function

We can also specify, in light of the nonmarket supply characteristics described in chapter 3, a heuristic supply function indicating the aggregate supply of nonmarket activities, as well as the component supply functions for particular nonmarket activities:

$$S_i = S_i (V_i, m_i, \sigma(T_i), P, R, Y)$$ (4)

and

$$S = \sum_1^n S_i,$$ (5)

where

S_i =   the supply of the ith nonmarket activity ($i = 1, 2, \ldots n$)

S =   the aggregate supply of the n activities (expressed in dollars of total input costs or budgets of the nonmarket activities)

V_i =   measurement accuracy of the ith nonmarket activity (V_i may be considered a qualitatively scaled variable reflecting the accuracy or precision with which the ith nonmarket product can be measured)

m_i =   degree of exclusivity (monopoly) characterizing the ith nonmarket activity[5]

$\sigma(T_i)$ =   the variance in the input/output relations associated with the technologies of nonmarket activities

P =   the cost of a "unit" of nonmarket input, as defined earlier

R =   the tax rate

Y =   national income

In accord with the preceding discussion, the partial derivatives associated with V_i and m_i are assumed to be, respectively, negative and positive. When agencies conduct nonmarket activities with the benefit of an imprecise measure of their performance, their supply costs (and budgets) S_i will also tend to be high.

Also, in accord with the preceding discussion, the partial derivatives associated with R, P, and Y are expected to be positive.

The partial derivative of nonmarket supply costs (budgets) with respect to the technological uncertainty of production, $\sigma(T_i)$, is also expected to be positive on the following grounds: A particular nonmarket activity, j, whose associated technology has a high variance ($\sigma(T) \rightarrow$ large), may consume substantial inputs while yielding little "final" (intended) output. On the other hand, if the cognizant agency is lucky, and the technology turns out to yield at least the intended output for less than budgeted costs, we assume the agency will tend to increase expenditures (e.g., by adding perquisites, featherbedding, or other means) to absorb the underrun. In the absence of profit as a maximand, the agency will at least measure up to its budget to avoid the penalty that often results from efficient nonmarket performance—namely, savings realized in *one* period often result in budget reductions in the next!

Nonmarket Equilibria and Nonmarket Failures

The framework previously developed suggests the possibility of equilibrium between particular and aggregate nonmarket demands and supplies. Three arguments are common to both demand and supply functions: the tax rate R; the nonmarket wage rate P; and national income Y. I have suggested that the slopes of R and P will be opposite in the two functions: negative in the aggregate nonmarket demand function and positive in the aggregate supply function.

Moreover, there is at least a general, if often weak, political process operating to correct divergences between nonmarket demands and supplies, in the aggregate and for particular types of nonmarket output. For example, if the demand for nonmarket activities resulting from equations (1) and (2) exceeds the supply resulting from equations (4) and (5), there will be a tendency in the political arena for P and/or R to rise (the Civil Service system and the Office of Personnel Management will be able to press for higher government salaries P, and the congressional finance and budget processes will be inclined to enact higher tax rates R), thereby tending to increase nonmarket supply, and reduce demand, in accord with the partial derivatives specified earlier. Conversely, if supply exceeds demand, there will be a (probably weak) tendency for elected officials and the political process to mediate the excess supply by lowering taxes and/or relative government pay scales, thereby moving down the S function and outward (southeast) on the D function, thus tending toward an equilibrium.

The income variable Y presents a problem. Not only are both nonmarket demand and supply functions likely to have positive slopes with respect to Y but, more important, there are likely to be multiple equilibria between the two functions in Y space. The political process can, not too unreasonably, be considered to mediate divergences between S and D: by adding programs, appropriations, and expenditures if there is excess demand or curtailing them if there is excess supply. But this process will go on, albeit weakly and imperfectly, at *all levels of income*, rather than defining a unique income level at which nonmarket demands and supplies are equilibrated.

In figure A.1, the hypothetical S and D functions cannot be regarded as defining a unique equilibrium at (S_e, D_e), (Y_e): Income will as likely be above or below the Y_e point. On either side of it the political process will operate, imperfectly and tardily, to bring nonmarket demand and supply toward convergence, as indicated by the arrows.

What about the arguments that are not common to the nonmarket demand and supply functions—namely, the perceived levels of externalities $\hat{X}$, monopoly $\hat{M}$, market imperfections $\hat{I}$, public goods demand $\hat{G}$, and inequities $\hat{E}$, in the nonmarket demand function; and the measurement accuracy V_i, exclusivity of nonmarket production m_i, and technological uncertainty $\sigma(T_i)$, in the nonmarket supply function? From the standpoint of the partial equilibrium context implied by the preceding discussion, these become shift variables that raise or lower the D and S functions to establish multiple and changing equilibria in the R, P, and Y space common to the two functions. In figure A.2, the

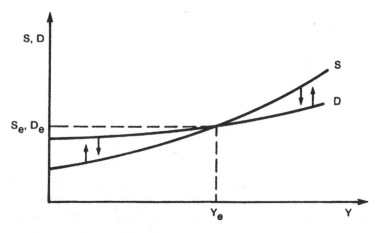

Figure A.1
Hypothetical nonmarket demand and supply functions.

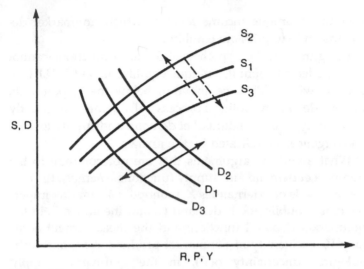

Figure A.2
Nonmarket equilibria and shift variables.

solid arrows represent the effect of the shift variables in the nonmarket demand function, and the broken-line arrows the effect of the shift variables in the nonmarket supply function. The nine intersections illustrate the multiple equilibria between nonmarket demand and supply in R, P, or Y space.

In a general equilibrium model, the shift variables would become endogenous, and a unique and stable equilibrium might be reached, or at least an equilibrium that is defined at each point in time. But general equilibrium is more a matter of pure mathematics and aesthetics than of the real and messy world of nonmarket demands and supplies. In this world, the equilibria are partial, multiple, and transitory, and the shift variables are more numerous, powerful, and changeable than the equilibrating ones. The most significant attribute of these partial equilibria is that they are all likely to be characterized by inefficiencies and inequities! The reason is that the nonmarket demands and supplies, whether in equilibrium or between equilibria, already embody inefficiencies or inequities—that is, nonmarket failures: Demand functions may be distorted by the perceptual characteristics of the shift variables; and supply functions may, for reasons discussed earlier, exhibit inflated costs without any reliable mechanism to realize technically feasible savings.

Notes

1. If v_{mj}^s represents the externalities experienced by all k individuals as a result of an individual i's consumption of the jth unit of a good s, then

$$X = \sum_{s=1}^{n} \sum_{m=i+1}^{k} v_{mj}^s ,$$ (3)

where n is the number of goods produced. x is the perceived magnitude of X.

2. For a discussion of the perplexing problem of defining and measuring equity, see Wolf (1981b).

3. There is some similarity between my treatment here of the demand for nonmarket activities and that of Buchanan (1969). For example, his point about the "functional relationship between quantity demanded and the 'tax price'" is the same as my comment about the negative partial derivative of D with respect to R. But thereafter our two arguments (in both meanings of the term) diverge.

4. Thus, $dD / dY = \delta D / \delta Y + (\delta R / \delta Y \cdot \delta D / \delta R)$. The expression in parentheses is the indirect tax-rate effect of income changes. It will provide a partial offset to the direct effect of income change on nonmarket demand ($\delta D / \delta Y > 0$), because $\delta R / \delta Y > 0$, and $\delta D / \delta R < 0$.

5. Note that m_i differs from M referred to in the demand function above: m_i refers to the degree of monopoly enjoyed by the nonmarket agency conducting the ith activity (in light of competing activites conducted elsewhere in the nonmarket sector or the market sector), whereas M refers to the degree of monopoly in the market sector.

Appendix B
A Survey of Comparisons between Public and Private Service Delivery

The following table is adapted, by permission, from Borcherding, Pommerehne, and Schneider (1982, 130–133) and from text discussion in Fitzgerald (1988) and Osborne and Gaebler (1992). Detailed references to the cited reports appear in the bibliography of the Borcherding monograph and in the text discussion in the Fitzgerald and the Osborne and Gaebler books.

Table B.1
Cost and productivity indices: alternative organizational forms

	Activity: Author	Unit/Organizational Forms	Findings
1.	**Airlines:** Davies (1971, 1977)	Australia/sole private domestic vs. its lone public counterpart.	Efficiency indices of private 12% to 100% higher.
2.	**Banks:** Davies (1982)	Australia/one public vs. one private bank.	Sign and magnitude of all indices of productivity, response to risk, and profitability favor private banks.
3.	**Bus service:** Oelert (1976)	Selected West German cities/municipal vs. private.	Cost per km of public bus service 160% higher than private equivalents.
4.	**Cleaning services:** Bundesrechnungshof (1972)	West German post offices/public production vs. private contracting-out.	Costs of public service 40% to 60% higher.
	Hamburger Senat (1971) Fischer-Menshausen (1975)	West German public buildings/public production vs. private contracting-out.	Costs of public service 50% higher than private alternative.
5.	**Debt collection:** Bennett and Johnson (1980)	U.S. General Accounting Office study/federal government-supplied service vs. privately contracted-for equivalents.	Government costs per dollar of debt pursued 200% higher.

Table B.1 (continued)

Activity: Author	Unit/Organizational Forms	Findings
6. Electric utilities:		
Meyer[a] (1975)	Sample of 60 to 90 U.S. utilities/public vs. private firms.	Weak indication of higher costs of private production.
Moore (1970)	Sample of U.S. utilities/27 municipal vs. 49 private firms.	Overcapitalization greater in public firms. Total operating costs of public production higher.
Spann[a] (1977)	Four major U.S. cities/public (San Antonio, Los Angeles) vs. private (San Diego, Dallas) firms.	Private firms adjusted for scale as efficient and probably more so with respect to operating cost and investment (per 1,000 kwh).
7. Environmental protection:		
Osborne and Gaebler (1992)	EPA introduced industrywide system of tradable permits among refiners for lead content reduction.	Program estimated by EPA to have saved 20% of the cost of reducing lead in gasoline.
8. Fire protection and prevention:		
Ahlbrandt (1973, 1974)	Selected U.S. areas/Scottsdale, Arizona (private contract) vs. Seattle area (municipal).	Cost per capita of municipal fire departments 39% to 88% higher.
Osborne and Gaebler (1992)	Scottsdale ordinance requiring sprinkler systems on every new building.	City saves 23% on infrastructure costs through reduced demands on fire department and equipment.

Table B.1 (continued)

	Activity: Author	Unit/Organizational Forms	Findings
9.	**Forestry:** Bundesregierung Deutschland (1976)	West Germany, 1965 to 1975/public vs. private forest harvesting.	Operating revenues in private forests DM 45 per hectare higher.
	Pfister (1976)	State of Baden-Wurttemberg/private vs. public forests.	Labor input twice as high per unit of output in public compared with private firms.
10.	**Hospitals and health care:** Clarkson (1972)	Sample of U.S. hospitals/private nonprofit vs. for-profit.	"Red tape" more prevalent in nonprofits. Greater variation in input ratios in nonprofits. Both suggest higher cost of nonprofit outputs.
	Lindsay[b] (1976)	Sample of U.S. hospitals/U.S. Veterans Administration (VA) vs. proprietary hospitals.	Cost per patient day less in VA hospital unadjusted for type of care and quality of less "serious" cases and longer patient stays in VA; preference for minority group professionals compared with proprietary hospitals.
	Rushing (1974)	Sample of 91 short-stay hospitals in U.S. mid-South region/private non-profits vs. for-profit.	Substitution among inputs and outputs more sluggish in nonprofit hospitals.

Table B.1 (continued)

Activity: Author	Unit/Organizational Forms	Findings
Wilson and Jadlow (1978)	1,200 U.S. hospitals producing nuclear medicine/government vs. proprietary hospitals.	Deviation of proprietary hospitals from perfect efficiency index less than public hospitals.
Osborne and Gaebler (1992)	San Francisco network of local clinics, hospices, welfare offices, and volunteers for AIDS patients.	City's average cost of AIDS treatment drops to 40% of national average.
	Florida state finances home care and community care for the elderly.	By keeping people out of nursing homes, the state saves $18 million a year.
Fitzgerald (1988)	Navarro County, Texas contracted with private health care firm to build and operate new hospital replacing one subsidized by county taxes.	Current tax revenues generated by facility at $300,000 annually, compared with $50,000 that county paid for operation of old hospital.
11. Housing: Muth (1973)	Construction costs in U.S. cities/private vs. public agencies.	Costs of public agencies 20% higher per constant quality housing unit.
Rechnungshof Rheinland-Pfalz (1972)	West German state of Rheinland-Pfalz/public vs. private costs of supplying large public building projects.	Costs of public agencies 20% higher than those of private contracting.
Schneider and Schuppener (1971)	West Germany/public vs. private firm construction costs.	Costs of public firms significantly higher.

Table B.1 (continued)

Activity: Author	Unit/Organizational Forms	Findings
12. **Insurance claims processing:** Frech (1976, 1979)	U.S. Social Security Administration contracting-out of Medicare claims/mutuals vs. proprietary insurance firms; mutuals vs. "other nonprofits" (largely Blue Shield) vs. proprietary insurance firms.	Mutuals 45% to 80% more costly than proprietary firms; mutuals are 22% more costly than proprietary insurance firms, but have 19% lower cost than "other nonprofits."
13. **Insurance sales and servicing:** Finsinger[a] (1981)	West Germany/five public vs. 77 private liability and life firms.	Same rate of return and no obvious cost differences between organizational forms.
Kennedy and Mehr (1977)	Selected Canadian samples/public car insurance in Manitoba vs. private insurance in Alberta.	Quality and services of private insurances higher than those of the public one.
14. **Military aircraft repair services and support:** Osborne and Gaebler (1992)	Vance Air Force Base contracting for aircraft repair and facilities operation.	Annual savings of $9 million, approximately 22% below the costs of comparable bases.
15. **Ocean tanker repair and maintenance:** Bennett and Johnson (1980)	U.S. General Accounting Office/Navy vs. commercial tankers and oilers.	U.S. Navy from 230% to 5100% higher.

Table B.1 (continued)

Activity: Author	Unit/Organizational Forms	Findings
16. Preschool education: Osborne and Gaebler (1992)	Arkansas training welfare mothers to educate their children at home 20 minutes daily.	After one year, children testing at or above national average jumped from 6% to 74%.
17. Railroads and mass transit: Caves and Christensen[a] (1980)	Canada/Canadian National (CN) (public) vs. Canadian Pacific (private).	No productivity differences recently, but CN less efficient before 1965, the highly regulated period.
Fitzgerald (1988)	Westchester County, New York continues to set fares and schedules, but contracts operation out to 11 private providers.	Service costs the county $3.26 per mile compared with neighboring county's costs of $4.27 per mile (ridership is roughly equal).
Fitzgerald (1988)	Dallas Area Rapid Transit contracted out citywide bus network to a three-firm consortium responsible for staffing maintenance and general management of the service.	City saves an estimated $9 million annually.
18. Refuse collection: Collins and Downes[a] (1977)	53 cities and municipalities in the St. Louis County area (Missouri)/public vs. private contracting-out modes.	No significant cost differences.

Table B.1 (continued)

Activity: Author	Unit/Organizational Forms	Findings
Columbia University Graduate School of Business Studies: Savas (1974, 1977a, 1977b, 1980) Stevens (1978) Stevens and Savas (1978) Edwards and Stevens (1976)	Many sorts of U.S. cities/municipal vs. private monopoly franchise vs. private nonfranchise firms.	Costs of public supply 40% to 60% higher than private, but monopoly franchise only 5% higher than private nonfranchise collectors.
Petrovic and Jaffee (1977)	83 cities in midwestern United States/public vs. private contracting-out modes.	Costs of city collectors 15% higher than those of private contract collectors.
Hirsch[a] (1965)	24 cities and municipalities in the St. Louis City-County area (Missouri)/public vs. private firms.	No significant cost differences.
Kemper and Quigley (1976)	101 Connecticut cities/private monopoly contract vs. private nonfranchise vs. municipal firms.	Municipal collection costs 14% to 43% higher than contract costs, but private nonfranchise 25% to 36% higher than municipal collection.
Kitchen (1976)	48 Canadian cities/municipal vs. private firms.	Municipal suppliers more costly than proprietary firms.
Savas[a] (1977c)	Minneapolis/50 private vs. 30 municipal firms.	No significant cost differences.
Pier, Vernon, and Wicks[b] (1974)	26 cities in Montana/municipal vs. private firms.	Municipal suppliers more efficient.

Table B.1 (continued)

Activity: Author	Unit/Organizational Forms	Findings
Pommerehne (1976)	102 Swiss municipalities/public vs. private firms.	Unit costs of public firms 15% higher.
Spann (1977)	Survey of various U.S. cities/municipal vs. private firms.	Costs of public firms 45% higher.
Bennett and Johnson (1979)	Fairfax County, Virginia/29 private firms vs. one public trash collection authority.	Private firms more efficient.
Osborne and Gaebler (1992)	Phoenix public-private sector bidding for collection service contracts.	City employees won back contracts for all regions of the city and reduced "real" costs by 4.5% per annum over 10-year period.
Osborne and Gaebler (1992)	Milwaukee Metropolitan Sewage District transforms sewage into fertilizer.	City realizes $7.5 million annually from the sale.
Osborne and Gaebler (1992)	Phoenix methane gas from wastewater treatment is sold to a neighboring city for home heating and cooking.	City earns $750,000 annually from this sale.
19. Removal of abandoned vehicles:		
Osborne and Gaebler (1992)	Chicago financed removal of abandoned vehicles by contracting.	City now receives $25 per car removed from contractor, instead of paying $24. Annual $2 million cost became $2 million revenue.

Table B.1 (continued)

	Activity: Author	Unit/Organizational Forms	Findings
20.	**Savings and loans:** Nichols (1967)	California savings and loans/cooperative or mutuals vs. stock companies.	Operating costs of mutuals 13 to 30% higher.
21.	**Slaughterhouses:** Pausch (1976)	Five major West German cities/private vs. public firms.	Costs of public firms significantly higher because of over-capacity and over-staffing.
22.	**Water utilities:** Crain and Zardkoohi (1978)	112 U.S. firms/municipal vs. private suppliers; case study of two firms who each switched organizational form.	Public firms 40% less productive with 65% higher capital-labor ratios than private equivalents; public firm that became private experienced an output per employee increase of 25%. Private firm that became public experienced an output per employee decline of 40%.
	Mann and Mikesell (1976)	U.S. firms/municipal vs. private suppliers.	Replicates Meyer's (1975) electricity model, with adjustment for input prices. Public modes 20% higher.
	Morgan (1977)	143 firms in six U.S. states/municipal vs. private suppliers.	Costs of public firms 15% higher.

Table B.1 (continued)

Activity: Author	Unit/Organizational Forms	Findings
23. **Weather forecasting:**		
Bennett and Johnson (1980)	U.S. General Accounting Office study/U.S. Weather Bureau vs. private contracted-for service.	Costs of government service 50% higher.

Sources: Partly taken from Blankart (1980a, table 7; 1980b) and other compilation from the literature.
a. No significant difference in costs or efficiencies.
b. Public sector less costly or more efficient.

Bibliography

Administrative Inspection Bureau, Management and Coordination Agency, "Privatization and Deregulation: The Japanese Experience," Tokyo, June 1990.

Advisory Commission on Intergovernmental Relations (ACIR), *Changing Public Attitudes on Governments and Taxes*, Washington, D.C., 1981.

Ahlbrandt, Roger S., *Municipal Fire Protection Services: Comparison of Alternative Organizational Forms*, Sage, Beverly Hills, Calif., 1973.

Alexander, Arthur J., *Armor Development in the Soviet Union and the United States*, RAND, R-1860-NA, April 1976.

Allison, Graham T., *Essence of Decision: Explaining the Cuban Missile Crisis*, Little, Brown & Co., Boston, Mass., 1971.

Allison, Graham T., "Implementation Analysis: The Missing Chapter in Conventional Analysis—A Teaching Exercise," in William Niskanen et al. (eds.), *Benefit-Cost and Policy Analysis*, Aldine, 1974.

Arrow, Kenneth J., The Organization of Economic Activity: Issues Pertinent to the Choice of Market versus Non-Market Allocation," in Robert Haveman and Julius Margolis (eds.), *Public Expenditure and Policy Analysis, Third Edition*, Houghton Mifflin, Boston, 1983.

Arrow, Kenneth J., "Political and Economic Evaluation of Social Effects and Externalities," in Michael D. Intriligator (ed.), *Frontiers of Quantitative Economics*, North-Holland, Amsterdam, 1971. Second title: "Contributions to Economic Analysis," Vol. 71.

Arrow, Kenneth J., *The Limits of Organization*, Norton, New York, 1974.

Averch, Harvey, and Leland L. Johnson, "Behavior of the Firm Under Regulatory Constraint," *American Economic Review*, Vol. 52, No. 1052, 1962.

Bacon, Robert William, and Walter A. Eltis, *Britain's Economic Problem: Too Few Producers*, MacMillan, London, 1976.

Bain, J. S., *Barriers to New Competition* (Harvard University Series on Competition in American Industry, No. 3) Harvard University Press, Cambridge, Mass., 1956.

Baldridge, Malcolm, "Rx for Export Woes: Antitrust Relief," *Wall Street Journal*, p. 32 (Western Ed.) or p. 28 (Eastern Ed.) 61.3, October 15, 1985.

Bator, Francis M., "The Anatomy of Market Failure," *Quarterly Journal of Economics*, Vol. 72, No. 351, 1958.

Bauer, P. T., *Reality and Rhetoric: Studies in the Economics of Development*, Harvard University Press, Cambridge, Mass., 1984.

Baumol, W. J., J. C. Panzar, and R. D. Willig, *Contestable Markets and the Theory of Industry Structure*, Harcourt Brace Jovanovich, San Diego, Calif., 1982.

Bell, Daniel, *The Coming of Post-Industrial Society*, Basic Books, New York, 1973.

Ben-Ner, Avner, and Theresa van Hoomissen, "Nonprofit Organizations in the Mixed Economy," *Annals of Public and Cooperative Economics*, Vol. 62, No. 4, 1991.

Ben-Ner, Avner, and Theresa van Hoomissen (eds.), *The Relative Size of the Nonprofit Sector in the Mixed Economy*, Strategic Management Research Center, University of Minnesota, 1990.

Berman, Paul, *The Study of Macro- and Micro-Implementation of Social Policy*, RAND, P-6071, January 1978.

Bernstam, Mikhail, "Trends in the Soviet Population and Labor Force Dynamics," in Henry S. Rowen and Charles Wolf, Jr. (eds.), *The Future of the Soviet Empire*, St. Martin's Press, New York, 1987.

Birdzell, L. Earl, "Business and Government: The Walls Between," in Neil H. Jacoby (ed.), *The Business-Government Relationship: A Reassessment*, Goodyear, Pacific Palisades, Calif., 1975.

Borcherding, Thomas E., Werner W. Pommerehne, and Friedrich Schneider, *Comparing the Efficiency of Private and Public Production: The Evidence from Five Countries*, Institute for Empirical Research in Economics, University of Zurich, Switzerland, 1982.

Bruck, Connie, "Strategic Alliances," *New Yorker*, Vol. 68, No. 20, 1992.

Bruer, John T., "Odds against Medical-School Admission Exaggerated," *New England Journal of Medicine*, Vol. 302, No. 18, p. 1036, May 1, 1980.

Buchanan, J. M., *Cost and Choice: An Inquiry in Economic Theory*, Markham, Chicago, Ill., 1969.

Buchanan, J. M., and G. Tullock, *The Calculus of Consent: Logical Foundations of Constitutional Democracy*, University of Michigan Press, Ann Arbor, 1962.

Bunce, Valerie, "Neither Equality Nor Efficiency: International and Domestic Inequalities in the Soviet Bloc," Chap. 1 in Daniel N. Nelson (ed.), *Communism and the Politics of Inequality*, D. C. Heath, Lexington, Mass., 1983.

Cairncross, Alexander, "The Market and the State," in Thomas Wilson and A. S. Skinner (eds.), *Essays in Honour of Adam Smith*, Oxford Clarendon Press, London, 1976.

Chubb, John, and Terry Moe, *Politics, Markets, and the Organization of Schools*, The Brookings Institution, Washington, D.C., 1986.

Coase, Ronald H., "The Problem of Social Cost," *Journal of Law and Economics*, Vol. 3, pp. 1–44, October 1960.

Coddington, Alan, "Creaking Semaphore and Beyond: A Consideration of Shackle's Epistemics and Economics," *British Journal of Philosophy of Science*, pp. 151–163, June 1975; cited in Brian Kantor, "Rational Expectations and Economic Thought," *Journal of Economic Literature*, December 1979.

Crecine, John P., *Research in Public Policy Analysis and Management*, Jai Press, Greenwich, Conn., 1981.

Cyert, Richard M., and James G. March, *A Behavioral Theory of the Firm*, Prentice-Hall, Englewood Cliffs, New Jersey, 1963.

Davis, J.R., and J. R. Hewlett, *An Analysis of Market Failure: Externalities, Public Goods, and Mixed Goods*, University of Florida Press, Gainesville, Fla., 1977.

DeBow, Michael E., "Markets, Government Intervention, and the Role of Information: An 'Austrian School' Perspective with an Application to Merger Regulation," *George Mason University Law Review*, Vol. 14, No. 1, Fall 1991.

Department of Commerce, *Procurement Programs*, National Technical Information Service, Springfield, Va., February 1991.

Downs, Anthony, *An Economic Theory of Democracy*, Harper & Row, New York, 1965.

Drucker, Peter F., *The Age of Discontinuity: Guidelines to Our Changing Society*, Harper & Row, New York, 1969.

Eby, Charles, *Performance Norms in Nonmarket Organizations: An Exploratory Survey*, RAND, N-1830-YALE, April 1982.

Federal Reserve Bank of San Francisco, *Airline Deregulation*, March 9, 1984.

Federal Reserve System, *Annual Statistics Digest, 1980–1989*, Board of Governors, Washington, D.C., 1990.

Feldstein, Martin, *Economic Analysis for Health Services Efficiency: Econometric Studies of the British National Health Service*, North-Holland, Amsterdam, 1968.

Feldstein, Martin, *The American Economy in Transition*, University of Chicago Press, 1980.

Feshbach, Murray, *The Soviet Union: Population Trends and Dilemmas*, Population Bulletin, Population Reference Bureau, 1982.

Feshbach, Murray, and Christopher Davis, *Rising Infant Mortality in the Soviet Union in the 1970s*, Bureau of the Census, Washington, D.C., 1980.

Fitzgerald, Randall, *When Government Goes Private: Successful Alternatives to Public Services*, Universe Books, New York, 1988.

Forte, F., and A. Peacock (eds.), *Public Expenditure and Government Growth*, Blackwell, Oxford and New York, 1985.

Friedman, Milton, *Tyranny of the Status Quo*, Harcourt Brace Jovanovich, New York, 1984.

Friedman, Milton, and Rose Friedman, *Free to Choose: A Personal Statement*, Harcourt Brace Jovanovich, New York, 1980.

Galbraith, John Kenneth, *Age of Uncertainty*, Houghton Mifflin, Boston, Mass., 1977.

Goeller, Bruce, Allan F. Abrahamse, James H. Bigelow, Joseph G. Bolten, David M. de Ferranti, James C. DeHaven, Thomas F. Kirkwood, and Robert L. Petruschell, *Policy Analysis of the Netherlands Oosterschelde*, RAND, R-2121/1-NETH, 1977.

Haldi, J., and D. Whitcomb, "Economies of Scale in Industrial Plants," *Journal of Political Economy*, Vol. 75, No. 4, Pt. I, pp. 373–385, August 1967.

Hall, M., and L. Weiss, "Firm Size and Profitability," *Review of Economics and Statistics*, Vol. 49, pp. 319–331, August 1967.

Hankla, James C., Chief Administrative Officer, Los Angeles County, *Report on Board Awarded Contracts*, Memorandum to the County Board of Supervisors, August 2, 1985.

Hargrove, Erwin C., *The Missing Link: The Study of Implementations of Social Policy*, The Urban Institute, Washington, D.C., 1975.

Harman, Alvin J., *Acquisition Cost Experience and Predictability*, RAND, P-4505, January 1971.

Head, Richard G., and Ervin J. Rokke, *American Defense Policy*, 3rd ed., John Hopkins Press, Baltimore, Md., 1973.

Heilbroner, Robert, "The Triumph of Capitalism," *New Yorker*, January 23, 1989.

Hirschman, Albert O., *Development Projects Observed*, The Brookings Institution, Washington, D.C., 1967.

Hirshleifer, Jack, James C. DeHaven, and Jerome W. Milliman, *Water Supply: Economics, Technology, and Policy*, University of Chicago Press, 1960.

Hodgkinson, Virginia A., and Murray S. Weitzman, *Dimensions of the Independent Sector: A Statistical Profile*, Independent Sector, Washington, D.C., 1984.

International Monetary Fund, *Government Financial Statistics Yearbook*, Washington, D.C., 1984.

International Monetary Fund, *Government Financial Statistics Yearbook*, Washington, D.C., 1991.

International Monetary Fund, *International Financial Statistics*, Washington, D.C., 1984.

International Monetary Fund, *International Financial Statistics*, Washington, D.C., 1991.

Kantor, Brian, "Rational Expectations and Economic Thought," *Journal of Economic Literature*, Vol. 17, No. 4, pp. 1421–1441, December 1979.

Keynes, John Maynard, *The General Theory of Employment Interest and Money*, Harcourt Brace, New York, 1936.

Krugman, Paul R., "Targeted Industrial Policies: Theory and Evidence," *Industrial Change and Public Policy*, Federal Reserve Bank of Kansas City, 1983.

Landau, Daniel, "Government Expenditure and Economic Growth: A Cross-Country Study," *Southern Economic Journal*, Vol. 49, No. 3, January 1983.

Leibenstein, Harvey, "Allocative Efficiency Versus X-Efficiency," *American Economic Review*, Vol. 56, No. 3, pp. 392–415, June 1966.

Lindblom, C. E., *Politics and Markets*, Basic Books, New York, 1977.

Lipsey, Richard G., and Kelvin Lancaster, "The General Theory of Second Best," *Review of Economic Studies*, Vol. 24, No. 11, 1956.

Little, I. M. D., *A Critique of Welfare Economics*, 2nd ed., Clarendon Press, Oxford, 1957.

March, James, G., and Herbert A. Simon, with the collaboration of Harold Guetzkow, *Organizations*, Wiley, New York, 1958.

Marsden, Keith, *Links between Taxes and Economic Growth: Some Empirical Evidence*, World Bank Staff Working Paper 605, Washington, D.C., 1983.

McFadden, Daniel, "The Revealed Preferences of a Government Bureaucracy: Theory," *Bell Journal of Economics*, Vol. 6, No. 401, 1975.

Merrow, Edward W., Stephen Chapel, and Christopher Worthing, *A Review of Cost Estimation in New Technologies*, RAND, R-2481-DOE, July 1979.

Mishan, E. J., "The Relationship between Joint Products, Collective Goods, and External Effects," *Journal of Political Economy*, Vol. 77, No. 329, 1969.

Moore, Frederick T., "Economies of Scale: Some Statistical Evidence," *Quarterly Journal of Economics*, Vol. 73, No. 2, pp. 232–245, May 1959.

Musgrave, Richard, *The Theory of Public Finance*, McGraw-Hill, New York, 1959.

Neels, Kevin, and Michael Caggiano, *The Entrepreneurial City*, RAND, R-3123-SP/FF, October 1984.

Newhouse, Joseph P., "Toward a Theory of Nonprofit Institutions: An Economic Model of a Hospital," *American Economic Review*, Vol. 60, No. 64, 1970.

Nicholson, Walter, *Microeconomic Theory*, Holt, Rinehart and Winston, Hinsdale, Ill., 1972.

Nimitz, Nancy, "Organization Motivations in Weapon Acquisition: Some Hypotheses," unpublished paper, 1975.

Niskanen, W. A., *Bureaucracy and Representative Government*, Aldine Atherton, Chicago, Ill., 1971.

Niskanen, W. A., "Bureaucrats between Self-Interest and Public Interest," in H. Hanusch (ed.), *Anatomy of Government Deficiencies*, Springer-Verlag, New York, 1983.

Office of Management and Budget, Office of Federal Procurement Policy, *Enhancing Governmental Productivity through Competition* (A Progress Report on OMB Circular A-76), June 1984.

Okun, Arthur, *Equality and Efficiency: The Big Trade-Off*, The Brookings Institution, Washington, D.C., 1975.

Olson, Mancur, *The Rise and Decline of Nations*, Yale University Press, New Haven, Conn., 1982.

Organization for Economic Cooperation and Development, *World Economic Outlook*, Paris, June 1992.

Organization for Economic Cooperation and Development (OECD), *Economic Outlook*, Paris, 1991.

Organization for Economic Cooperation and Development, *The Role of the Public Sector*, Paris, 1985.

Osborne, David, and Ted Gaebler, *Reinventing Government: How the Entrepreneurial Spirit is Transforming the Public Sector*, Addison-Wesley, Reading, Mass., 1992.

Palfry, T., and T. Romer, "Warranties, Performance, and the Resolution of Buyer-Seller Disputes," *Bell Journal of Economics*, Vol. 14, No. 1, pp. 97–117, Spring 1983.

Pascal, Anthony H., *Clients, Consumers, and Citizens, Using Market Mechanisms for the Delivery of Public Services*, RAND, P-4803, March 1972.

Pascal, Anthony H., Michael N. Caggiano, Judith C. Fernandez, Kevin F. McCarthy, Kevin Neels, C. Peter Rydell, and James P. Stucker, *Equitable Beneficiary-Based Finance in Local Government*, RAND, R-3124-HHS/SP/FF, June 1984.

Peacock, Alan, *The Economic Analyses of Government and Related Theories*, St. Martin, New York, 1980.

Perroux, Francois, *Theorie Generale du Progres Economique*, Vol. II, Paris, 1957.

Peters, Tom, and Nancy K. Austin, *A Passion for Excellence*, Random House, New York, 1985.

Peyrefitte, Alain, *Le Mal Français*, Plon, Paris, 1976.

Posner, Richard A., "Theories of Economic Regulation," *Bell Journal of Economics and Management Science*, Vol. 5, No. 335, 1974.

Pressman, Jeffrey L., and Aaron Wildavsky, *Implementation: How Great Expectations in Washington Are Dashed in Oakland; or, Why It's Amazing that Federal Programs Work at All*, University of California Press, Berkeley, 1973.

Pryor, Frederic L., "Growth and Fluctuations of Production in OECD and East European Countries," *World Politics*, January 1985.

Rawls, John, *A Theory of Justice*, Belknap Press, Cambridge, Mass., 1971.

Reder, Melvin W., *Studies in the Theory of Welfare Economics*, AMS Press, New York, 1947.

Relman, Arnold S., "Dealing with Conflicts of Interest," *New England Journal of Medicine*, Vol. 313, No. 12, pp. 749–751, September 19, 1985.

Rice, Donald B., "The Potentialities of Public Policy Research," in Neil H. Jacoby (ed.), *The Business-Government Relationship: A ReassessmentProceedings of a Seminar at the Graduate School of Management*, University of California Press, Los Angeles, 1975.

Rich, Michael, and Edmund Dews, *Improving the Military Acquisition Process*, RAND, R-3373-AF/RC, February 1986.

Rogerson, William P., *Overhead Allocation and Incentives for Cost Minimization in Defense Procurement*, RAND, R-4013-PA&E, 1992.

Rogerson, William P., *An Economic Framework for Analyzing DoD Profit Policy*, RAND, R-3860-PA&E, 1992.

Rogozinski, Jacques, "Learning the ABCs of Mexico's Privatization Process," *The Wall Street Journal*, May 15, 1992.

Roper Center for Public Opinion Research, University of Connecticut, Storrs, Conn., 1991.

Ross, Randy L., *Choosing Roles and Missions for Government and the Private Sector: A Preliminary Framework and Analysis*, RAND, N-2215-SF, November 1984.

Ross, Randy L., *Government and the Private Sector: Who Should Do What?* Taylor & Francis, New York, 1988.

Rothman, Stanley, and Robert S. Lichter, "Elites in Conflict: Nuclear Energy and the Perception of Risk," *Journal of Contemporary Studies*, Vol. 8, No. 3, Summer/Fall 1985.

Samuelson, Paul A., "The Pure Theory of Public Expenditure," *Review of Economics and Statistics*, Vol. 36, No. 387, 1954.

Sapolsky, Harvey, *The Polaris System Development: Bureaucratic and Programmatic Success in Government*, Harvard University Press, Cambridge, Mass., 1972.

Savas, E. S., *Privatizing the Public Sector*, Chatham House, Chatham, New Jersey, 1982.

Scherer, F. M., *Industrial Market Structure and Economic Performance*, Rand McNally, Chicago, Ill., 1970.

Schlesinger, James R., "Systems Analysis and the Political Process," *Journal of Law and Economics*, Vol. 11, pp. 281–298, October 1968.

Schultze, Charles L., *The Public Use of Private Interest*, The Brookings Institution, Washington, D.C., 1977.

Schumpeter, J. A., *The Theory of Economic Development*, Harvard University Press, Cambridge, Mass., 1934.

Scitovsky, Tibor, "The State of Welfare Economics," *American Economic Review*, Vol. 41, No. 303, 1951.

Sidgwick, Henry, *Principles of Political Economy*, MacMillan, London, 1887.

Simon, Herbert A., *The New Science of Management Decision*, Harper & Row, New York, 1960.

Spann, Robert M., "Public versus Private Provision of Government Services," in Thomas E. Borcherding (ed.), *Budgets and Bureaucrats: The Sources of Governmental Growth*, Duke University Press, Durham, North Carolina, 1977.

Stevens, Barbara J. (ed.), *Delivering Municipal Services Efficiently: A Comparison of Municipal and Private Service Delivery*, prepared for the U.S. Department of Housing and Urban Development by Ecodata, Inc., New York, June 1984.

Stigler, George, "The Theory of Economic Regulation," *Bell Journal of Economics and Management Science*, Vol. 2, No. 3, 1971.

Stockfisch, Jack A., *Analysis of Bureaucratic Behavior: The Ill-Defined Production Process*, RAND, P-5591, January 1976.

Summers, Robert, *Cost Estimates as Predictors of Actual Weapons Costs: A Study of Major Hardware Articles*, RAND, RM-3061-PR (abridged), March 1965.

Sze, Man-Bing, *Pension Funding Policy and Corporate Finance*, Ph.D. dissertation, The RAND Graduate School, Santa Monica, Calif., May 1985.

Tew, Bernard V., J. M. Broder, and W. M. Musser, "Market Failure in Multi-Phase Irrigation," *American Journal of Agricultural Economics*, Vol. 64, No. 5, 1982.

Thurow, Lester, "Psychic Income: A Market Failure," *Journal of Post-Keynesian Economics*, pp. 183–193, Winter 1981.

Universal Health Care Almanac, Silver & Cherner, Ltd., Phoenix, Ariz., 1992, Table 1.9.1.

Viner, Jacob, *The Customs Union Issues*, Carnegie Endowment for International Peace, 1950.

Viner, Jacob, "The Intellectual History of Laissez Faire," *Journal of Law and Economics*, Vol. 3, pp. 45–69, October 1960.

Vishnevskaya, Galina, *Galina: A Russian Story*, Guy Daniels, translated from Russian, Harcourt Brace Jovanovich, San Diego, Calif., 1984.

von Hayek, Frederich, "Competition as a Discovery Procedure," in Chiaki Nishiyama and Kurt R. Leube, *The Essence of Hayek*, Hoover Institution Press, Stanford, Calif., 1984.

Voslensky, Michael, *Nomenklatura: The Soviet Ruling Class*, Doubleday, Garden City, New York, 1984.

Weintraub, Sidney, *Price Theory*, Pitman, 1949.

Weitzman, Martin, *The Shared Economy: Conquering Stagflation*, Harvard University Press, Cambridge, Mass., and London, 1984.

Williamson, Oliver, *The Economic Institutions of Capitalism*, The Free Press, New York, 1985.

Wolf, Charles, Jr., "A Theory of Nonmarket Failure," *Journal of Law and Economics*, Vol. 22, No. 1, pp. 107–139, April 1979 (1979a).

Wolf, Charles, Jr., "Economic Efficiency and Inefficient Economics," *Journal of Post-Keynesian Economics*, Vol. 2, No. 1, pp. 79–82, Fall 1979 (1979b).

Wolf, Charles, Jr., "Economic Success, Stability, and the 'Old' International Economic Order," *International Security*, Vol. 6, No. 1, Summer 1981 (1981a).

Wolf, Charles, Jr., "Ethics and Policy Analysis," in J. Fleishman, L. Liebman, and M. Moore (eds.), *Public Duties: The Moral Obligations of Government Officials*, Harvard University Press, Cambridge, Mass., 1981 (1981b).

Wolf, Charles, Jr., "Getting to Market," *The Public Interest*, pp. 43–50, Spring 1991.

Wolf, Charles, Jr., "Government Shortcomings and the Conditions of Demand," in H. Hanusch (ed.), *Public Finance and the Quest for Efficiency: Proceedings of the 38th Congress of the International Institute of Public Finance, Copenhagen 1982*, Wayne State University Press, Detroit, Mich., 1984.

Wolf, Charles, Jr., "Management Without a 'Bottom Line,'" unpublished paper, 1982.

Wolf, Charles, Jr., "'Non-Market Failure' Revisited: The Anatomy and Physiology of Government Deficiencies," in H. Hanusch (ed.), *Anatomy of Government Deficiencies*, Springer-Verlag, New York, 1983.

Wolf, Charles, Jr., "SDI Is No Economic Elixir," *Wall Street Journal*, p. 36, October 24, 1985.

Wolf, Charles, Jr., William R. Harris, Robert E. Klitgaard, John R. Nelson, and John P. Stein, *Pricing and Recoupment Policies for Commercially Useful Technology Resulting from NASA Programs*, RAND, R-1671-NASA, January 1975.

Wolf, Charles, Jr., K. C. Yeh, Donald Henry, James Hayes, John Schank, and Richard Sneider, *The Changing Balance: South and North Korean Capabilities for Long-Term Military Competition*, RAND, R-3305/1-NA, December 1985.

Xinhua (Chinese News Agency), *Proposal of the Central Committee of the Chinese Communist Party for the Seventh Five-Year Plan for National Economic and Social Development*, Beijing, September 25, 1985.

Index